PLANTS, ANDROIDS AND OPERATORS

EDITED BY
CLEMENS APPRICH, JOSEPHINE BERRY SLATER,
ANTHONY ILES & OLIVER LERONE SCHULTZ

A collaboration between the Post-Media Lab
& Mute Books

Mute

Anti copyright © 2014 Mute

Except for those images which originally appeared elsewhere and are republished here, all content is copyright Mute and the authors. However, Mute encourages the use of its content for purposes that are non-commercial, critical, or disruptive of capitalist property relations. Please make sure you credit the author and Mute as the original publishers.

This legend is devised in the absence of a licence which adequately represents the contributors' and publishers' respective positions on copyright, and to acknowledge but deny the copyrighting performed by default where copyright is waived.

Please email mute@metamute.org with any details of republication
Co-published as a collaboration between Mute and the Post-Media Lab, Leuphana University. PML Books is a book series accompanying the work of the Post-Media Lab. http://postmedialab.org

Print ISBN: 978-1-906496-96-8
Also available as eBook: 978-1-906496-97-5

Distribution Please contact mute@metamute.org for trade and distribution enquiries

Acknowledgements

Series Editors Clemens Apprich, Josephine Berry Slater, Anthony Iles & Oliver Lerone Schultz
Layout Raquel Perez de Eulate
Design Template Based on a template by Atwork
Cover Design Sina Hurnik
Cover Photo Lilian Wagdy, Kairo 2 Dec 2011

PML Books

The books in this short series are:

Claire Fontaine, *Human Strike Has Already Begun & Other Writings*, (ISBN 978-1-906496-88-3)

Felix Stalder, *Digital Solidarity*, (ISBN 978-1-906496-92-0)

Clemens Apprich, et. al., *Provocative Alloys: A Post-Media Anthology*, (ISBN 978-1-906496-94-4)

V.M., *Irational.org's Traum: A Psychoarchaeological Dramaturgy*, (ISBN 978-1-906496-98-2)

Rodrigo Nunes, *The Organisation of the Organisationless: The Question of Organisation After Networks*, (ISBN 978-1-906496-75-3)

The PML Book series is just one of several outlets for the Lab's exploration of post-media strategies and conditions, which includes fellowships, a virtual lab structure, multiple collaborations, events, group readings and other documentation.

For more information see: www.postmedialab.org/publications

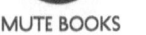
MUTE BOOKS

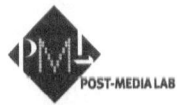
PML Books

The Post-Media Lab is part of the Lüneburg Innovation Incubator, a major EU project within Leuphana University of Lüneburg, financed by the European Regional Development Fund and co-funded by the German federal state of Lower Saxony.

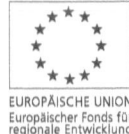
EUROPÄISCHE UNION
Europäischer Fonds für regionale Entwicklung

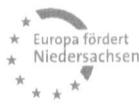
Europa fördert Niedersachsen

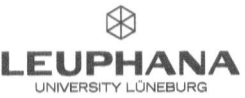
LEUPHANA
UNIVERSITY LÜNEBURG

CONTENTS

Preface
Clemens Apprich, Josephine Berry Slater, Anthony Iles &
Oliver Lerone Schultz..6

Digital Networks: Connecting People Apart 13

**Mahalla, Manalaa, Tahrir, Maspero: Post-Media Nodes
of the Egypt Spring**
A conversation between Oliver Lerone Schultz & Mina Emad 16

Process Processed
Josephine Berry Slater 32

The Subsumption of Sociality 39

Notes on Subsumption
Anthony Iles.. 42

**Destructive Destruction – An Ecological Study of High
Frequency Trading**
Inigo Wilkins & Bogdan Dragos 54

Field Notes from the Cloud
Sean Dockray... 70

Seamlens
Gordan Savičić 80

The Question of Organisation After Networks 87

Immanence After Networks
Rózsa Zita Farkas 90

Movements of Safety, A Safety Movement, Safety in Movement
Micha Cárdenas 114

Click Social Activism? A Localisation of Political Participation After Networks
Moritz Queisner..126

Life vs. Object, Comrade Things and Alien Life 139

Mapping the Conjecture
Fabien Giraud 142

Stack, Heap, Frame
Martin Howse & Jonathan Kemp 158

Deckspace.TV reSynced
Adnan Hadzi & James Stevens 168

Contributors Biographies 183

PREFACE

CLEMENS APPRICH, JOSEPHINE BERRY SLATER,
ANTHONY ILES & OLIVER LERONE SCHULTZ

The Post-Media Lab's first life-cycle, which this book documents, ran from September 2011 to February 2014. Its focus was the potential for 'post-media' practices. Its inspiration and name are derived from Félix Guattari's concept of those social and media assemblages which unleash new forms of collective expression and experience. Retrieving Guattari's concept of post-media, which can be found running through 30 years of new media practice and theory, the Post-Media Lab (PML) offered a space in which to reflect and operate upon the networked, mediatised society. Not regarding this as a purely theoretical endeavour, it also drew on the provocative notion of 'post-media operators' developed by Howard Slater through which he linked mediatised (sub-)cultures of all sorts with a programmatics of non-conformist practice.

The PML's activity was centred around a supported programme of visiting fellows – artists, activists, technologists, film-makers, theorists and post-media operators – and the production of a series of associated, international public events and publishing projects. Fellows were invited to join one of four research themes organised in six-month cycles. The themes formed the spine through which related events took shape and therefore also structure the chapters of this book. They are: Digital Networks: Connecting People Apart; The Subsumption of Sociality; The Question of Organisation After Networks; and Life vs. Object, Comrade Things and Alien Life.

As an accompaniment to the fellowship programme and a means to develop its themes in writing, PML co-published a book series together with Mute Books. Claire Fontaine's *The Human Strike Has Already Begun & Other Writings* looked at subsumed subjectivity as the fundamental ground of political resistance. Felix Stalder's *Digital Solidarity* considered how networks remake social struggle and influence social change. Irational.org's *Traum: A Psychoarchaeologist's Dramaturgy* by the eponymous art collective explored, in multiple fictional registers, the relationship between the administrative, technological, curatorial and emotional conditions of (net)art. And Rodrigo Nunes' *Organisation of the Organisationless* took on the question of how global social movements *move* within networks. Alongside this central axis of activity, the Post-Media Lab also engaged in different events, like Video Vortex #9, and other longer term co-operations. In particular our ongoing work with the transmediale/reSource programme, (sustained with great care by Tatiana Bazzichelli), and a whole ecosystem of Latin-American post-media networks (labSurlab, metareciclagem, Tropixel) all deserve mention.

In the 'post-media era', different content carriers (text, image, audio) recombine in original and unpredictable ways under the levelling organisation of networked computing that redefines the specificities of each medium. 'Post-media' as a concept was also formulated in antagonism with the emerging framework of post-modernism in the early-1990s, in its emphasis on the production of singularities within conditions of equivalence. It was then revived for the network era in the late-1990s and early-2000s, and for a reconfigured landscape of global geopolitics. To consider the term in its historical development and contemporary vectors, the Lab's first publishing endeavour was the compilation of an anthology eventually published as *Provocative Alloys: A Post-Media Anthology*. A book which brings together early forecasts of post-media practice with analysis by the post Web 2.0 generation, creating rich entanglements of theory, history and practice.

With the growing ubiquity of digital media ushered in by the '90s 'web revolution', and the rise of the 'invisible computer', one might assume that today we are all 'post-media operators'. But this 'media becoming' has in fact rendered the underlying technical and social processes ever more invisible, or at least beyond easy reach. Once again, we are in danger of the media enunciating us, of becoming the media-operated, in tune with the usual doxologies of power. Politically, post-media encourages the building and association of autonomous forms of collectivity within an exploded cultural environment. Such operations release multiple, singularising energies that conflict with hierarchy and centralised monoform broadcast culture in a given local and geopolitical frame.

Our idea was not to simply do research, but to make things, situations, devise tactics, create enunciations. Building apps, making art, developing activist campaigns, writing theory or engineering systems should not happen in isolation but be connected as hybrid practices. Nevertheless, a lot of our output did fall into the categories of production and thought we had initially eschewed, like exhibitions, books and conferences. This division of production was offset, to some degree, by the way we worked across activities in the Lab, so that art exhibitions were curated by activists, artists and philosophers debated tech with hackers, and amateurs became archivists, etc. The diverse specialisms of the participants in each research phase meant that the Lab never fell into one kind of practice. The Lab aimed to build a place where the aesthetic and utopian moments of ubiquitous media could be retrieved, and the multilayered forces and textures of media space were made newly legible. We took up 'post-media' as an inherently critical notion adequate to the media strategies of scenes, movements and collectives – rather than the individualities and normativities produced by commercial media. In the midst of another wave of hype and massification of network-based technologies, the term seemed to provide a position of criticality over the aggregation of small actors by large monopolies, infrastructural land grabs and powerful private-public institutions.

This tension between the utopian thinking animating the Lab and the limits imposed by the real conditions it unfolded within was also an effect of its funding criteria and the administrative logic we were enmeshed in. The Post-Media Lab was housed within a regional development incubator, funded by the European Regional Development Fund and the State of Lower Saxony. Situated within an EU-funded regional development project at a growing German university, the Lab could be seen as symptom of the European-wide restructuring of education after the Bologna Process.[1] However, the contradiction between the neoliberal hunger for creativity and knowledge development, and its imposition of conditions that attack this inventiveness at its very roots – the pervasive logic of the market – is one that globally afflicts culture, education and 'knowledge creation'. The fact that Leuphana University has used its EU funding to reinvent itself in the guise of what E.P. Thompson once dubbed the 'Business University' is just a local iteration of this ubiquitous logic. If the Post-Media Lab critically engaged this wider landscape in which education and creative practices are subsumed into the logic and form of the market, it did so whilst knowing very well that its own creative and critical labour was always-already precuperated as fodder for indicators, productivity metrics, place branding and reputation economy. Whilst acknowledging that the Lab was not exactly Guattari's Radio Alice during Bologna's hot spring of '77, or the micro-labs that erupted across Europe in the 1990s, (of which Backspace provides an iconic example in this book), this condition of subsumption is also the generalised one in which any and all progressive or resistant thought must find its fissures of opportunity.[2]

The Lab and its fellows created many memorable moments in which it felt like the psychic container of institutionalisation started to open up. With heartening frequency, dry theoretical conceptions of certain social, political and technical conditions were pierced by the passionate and often self-risking commitment of diverse practitioners. We experienced this in our discussions with Marcell Mars about his attempts to build a truly Public Library at the HAIP festival in Ljubljana (2012). Or Anne Roth's account of her mounting involvement in privacy campaigns at a conference examining the relationship between social media and social activism at Leuphana University (2011). Or irational.org's construction of a woodland data processing bureau built with wood, charcoal and fire, on the Lüneburg Heath during their Anarchaeology of an Artserver exhibition, December 2013, which worked to break down the assumed neutrality or normalcy of our high-tech world. Or Harry Sanderson's chilling anatomisation of the violence inherent in high-resolution images which caused the weightless slickness of our mediascape to give way, revealing instead a picture of global human and resource exploitation. Or the widening of our geo-political horizons sparked by our exchanges with Aniara Rodado, Felipe Fonseca, Alejo Duque and Karla Brunet that we were lucky enough to experience on both sides of the Atlantic.

Throughout the Lab's course, consistent attention was paid not only to new technologies and their effects but also to the material strata underpinning the intensification of life and work at one end of the 'Big-Data' pipes. If this is evident in this volume (Inigo Wilkins' & Bogdan Dragos' research into high-frequency trading, Sean Dockray's 'fieldnotes from the cloud' and Martin Howse & Jonathan Kemp's computational land art projects), it also permeated many of the conversations and projects from the very beginning of the Lab to the end. Such strata could be glimpsed in early conversations with Graswurzel.tv about mapping brown coal mining (and the resistances this creates), in irational.org's data archaeological activities, and our final closing conference, Taking Care of Things. The looming environmental question and the intractability of material, human and energetic limits to the current state of technology remains a major challenge to the uncritical optimism surrounding the digital. However, the political ambiguity of what *is* possible through new combinations of subjects around and through media will continue to be meaningfully probed in post-media practice. As the Post-Media Lab, we hope to have contributed something to this collective endeavour.

Underpinning the knowledge commons is a tremendous amount of hard work and emotional expenditure. It is therefore appropriate to take this opportunity to thank all who took part and contributed to the Lab over its brief but intense first phase.

Recalling all agents!

Footnotes

1   The Post-Media Lab was a collaboration between *Mute* and Leuphana University, Lüneburg in the context of MANEC – Media Art: Network and Cluster Creation in the Media at Leuphana University, Lüneburg. MANEC itself sits within the Digital Media Centre of the Innovation-Incubator Lüneburg, a research initiative mainly funded by the European Fund for Regional Development. Aside from this institutional set-up, the Post-Media Lab brought together four different trajectories and biographies in the shape of its co-ordinators, as well as traditions of (Central-European) activism.
2   See, Adnan Hadzi & James Stevens, 'Deckspace.TV reSynced diaries', pp.168-181.

DIGITAL NETWORKS: CONNECTING PEOPLE APART

The pronouncements of early web and new media enthusiasts were laden with the dreams and language of (re)forging community on the digital frontier. These days, though, we tend to hear more about 'community managers' and 'herding' than virtual communities, cybersalons or digital cities. Where communities of the '90s often owned their own networks, today's social media platforms own the infrastructure and, by extension, the communities which inhabit them. What happened to those early visions, what were their limits, how were they abandoned, and what are the implications of our transition into the more abstract field of mass internet use and media society 2.0?

The propulsive feedback between street demonstrations and/or insurrections and networked transmission indicate the profound disillusionment over the net's direct democratic effects to have been premature – at least where a direct causality is sought. Yet the potential reach of user friendly tools that have brought the masses onto the internet stage and networked media interfaces that surround us are equally amenable to the imperatives of commerce and government.

If the internet provides an interface to populations and their management, we can also see it as an agile space filled by numberless connections, communities and mass ingenuity; passifying platforms, like Facebook, can be temporarily hijacked for demos-founding actions one step ahead of punitive governmental action. Nation states are feeling the pressure and distortions of digital networks as their sovereignty is threatened by the volatility of financial markets and copycat waves and forms of protest. In this research phase, the Lab will think through the tensions between the principles of universal access and openness, the exclusivity and languages/grammars of virtual communities and radical milieus, and the impersonality and abstraction of mediatised network society. Research fellows are asked to consider and engage with the confusingly contradictory use of a technical assemblage which connects and alienates, gives rise to riots and hegemonic control, voices polyphony and imposes monoform.

MAHALLA, MANALAA, TAHRIR, MASPERO: POST-MEDIA NODES OF THE EGYPT SPRING

A CONVERSATION BETWEEN
OLIVER LERONE SCHULTZ &
MINA EMAD

Oliver Lerone Schultz met Mina Emad, a media artist from Cairo who has worked extensively with artivist engagements in the context of Hosni Mubarak's Egypt, in November 2011. The conversation took place just before the second Tahrir movement which developed in the build up to parliamentary elections after Mubarak had stepped down – and with renewed repression and restoration already in view. The edited transcript was amended with some further contextual and updated information (footnotes) to better situate it's somewhat 'historical' content, also in light of later developments.

Political Spaces: Birth of a Blogosphere

OLIVER LERONE SCHULTZ: How did you become immersed in political and media-related activism in Egypt?

MINA EMAD: Back in 2006 I decided to engage with the then non-existent Egyptian political scene. I mean a scene that I couldn't be part of because there was no space really before that. And so it was only in certain spaces, certain very tiny spaces that people were necessarily called activists – because they were outside the mainstream official parties, which were not really opposition parties they were just hollow parties, so you had to be on the very margins and there were very few. And at the time in 2005/2006, even later, when actions would be called for, they turned out to be very small. And it would always be the same 50 or 60 people who would be going, doing stand- or sit-ins surrounded by 500 riot police.

So there was no space or especially not on the official political scene and not in the city or in the streets. So the only space that one could find was the internet. And so that's when blogs started to become popular and a whole new generation of Egyptians ran into that space; growing slowly and meshing itself into becoming a reality, a reality big enough that it could make decisions, discuss topics, increase the size of gatherings, share information. There was an excellent initiative created at this time: Manalaa, which was a blog aggregator.[1] That was done by a man who is actually now in jail. After nine months of revolution the military is still cracking down on the freedom of expression.[2] His name is Alaa Abd El-Fattah and he and his wife Manal Hassan had created this aggregator which allowed us to see the growth of our 'bloggosphere' and made it possible for you to connect information, and all sort of initiatives, people, writing and even poetry, or calls for an event for a flash mob, sharing data, banners and so on.

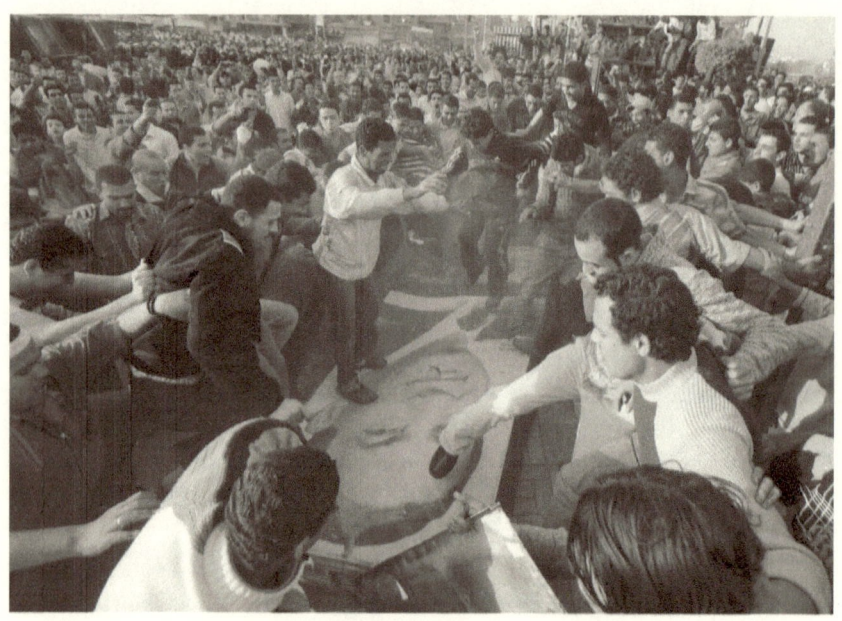
Mahalla Strikers trampling a Mubarak poster.
Photo by Hossam el-Hamalawy, Mahalla, 14 April 2008

So, there was a space created on the internet and this was our space, it was free.[3] And that's when I engaged with this space and tried to make the most out of it too, before Twitter and Facebook. It was open, uncensored – and it was risky because some bloggers were traced by IP and internet addresses, and the security services would knock at their door and throw them in jail.[4]

Internet Rising – Medium of the Masses

So I developed this strategy based on total anonymity.[5] The internet, especially at that time was very small. Maybe 10 percent of the population was accessing it at the time. Today it's 40 to 60 percent, or more.

OLS: What was the role of internet connectivity in these political developments?

ME: It depends really when we're looking at it. So let's say till 2007/8 we're talking about an internet where Facebook and Twitter are not really playing a decisive role. It's only after that. Then Twitter becomes almost like a telephone device: it's like mass communication, being someone somewhere talking to many, giving their views on something, describing, sharing images and so on. It's an amazing source of direct information. And it's faster than anything. Before it's even hit the television, you already have the footage itself! You have the information, the description, the location and everything – so it's like a pre-print in the press.

It was this type of curve: slow in the beginning, and then suddenly a spike. So the very slow went from 2000 to 2002. But it's really in 2010 or 2011 that it just went up through the roof, because it became a national concern. Before it was just a microcosm of microcosms of people; but then everybody was carrying the cause until it became huge.

UnDead Symbols, Social Images + Creeping Publics

OLS: How can we imagine the intersectionality of these different social processes at that time?

ME: One of the moments when it became bigger was with this other symbolic event with the death of Kahled Saheed, the young man who was beaten to death by police in Alexandria. And this shocked the entire population, it was in the press. It was taken up by the young activists who took it as a symbol and started innovating ways of claiming public space, in a way that could not breach the emergency laws which forbade that we gathered, forbade that we move the reunion in the street and so on. So there were flash mobs that were organised in Alexandria along the sea where everybody wore black, and just stood three meters away from each other looking at the horizon, and that was a very beautiful image.[6] And it was another type of strategy to be together, to take the streets but in a way that can't be attacked by the authorities.

Everything worked separately and together, there were things chronologically that had nothing to do with the blogosphere. For example, the workers' movements: they weren't triggered by the blogosphere but they were followed and magnified by the blogosphere. One of the most important youth movements, called the '6th of April Movement', has taken its name from a workers' strike that it did not organize itself, but that it considered as a major event in Egypt's recent history. Because what happened in Mahalla in 2007/08 was very promising in terms of confronting the authorities, taking down Mubarak's portraits, throwing stones at police cars, burning police cars and so on; taking the streets, occupying Mahalla, the whole city, so that was definitely a big symbol.[7] But at the time not everybody was quite aware of what had really happened. No footage, no images. Reporters were being stopped before arriving to Mahalla. It was very meticulous, how information is concealed.

Confluence – 25 Jan

Then we also had the socialist movements, or bloggers that were very much concerned by the workers' situation. I'm thinking in particular of someone like Hossam el-Hamalawy, who was monitoring the situation amazingly.[8] About seven or eight years it has been going on – in the factories, in all of the provinces, and he was documenting strike after strike and building up an archive of workers' movements in Egypt and this is extremely concrete; this is not Facebook, this is not new media, it has nothing to do with that. It's just what it is: people who work, the economy which is bad, and these simply true claims.

So before 25 January 2011, you had a certain 'class' of activists, who were very involved, who were connected and so on. Now the millions of people who came down to the streets on that day had no idea that these people existed. It is actually afterwards when these same voices were being introduced, being known better, leading certain initiatives that the rest of the population realised there was the 'underworld' that they'd never heard of, that was never discussed. And although there would be a lot of campaigns and someone would be arrested, you would never hear about them at the level of national media. So these were like two separate worlds whose intentions coincided on 25 January.

I think the Khaled Saheed issue was the most prominent event that maybe shed some light on the existence of all these movements, these activists and so on. But really everything was actually separate, and off 'the radar'. I think one of the common grounds, one of the common denominators was basic human rights. This was the ground to political awakening or at least struggle. And it's a huge issue in Egypt because there is a constant violation of human rights on all levels.

Revolution as Media Infection

OLS: To what extent was media coverage playing out in all this?

ME: I think it was very important because the activists were very aware of all that has been going on in Tunisia and also elsewhere in other places and so on. I think it might be the first time in this part of the world that all TV channels show the fall, or the fall in the making, of an Arab dictator. And these kids were young, you know, 'They look like our neighbours', and so, 'Oh, it's possible!'[9] So this was the first time that this type of image was diffused, broadcast on television.

OLS: It was also on Egyptian state television?

ME: Yes, I mean it was up on all the TV stations and all over the news and this was something the government could not control. Maybe had they thought, they would have controlled it, just like China forbids access to the images of Tiananmen Square. I think they were taken a bit off guard with these images. They know what the impact of these images can be because they have forbidden them for so long; every single image, every single article, every single word would be censored because they know the tremendous impact. And yet it happened.

OLS: And Al Jazeera?

ME: Al Jazeera had an open camera 24 hours a day and so it wasn't even edited material, it was just a flow, a constant flow of live transmission, which of course annoyed the authorities tremendously because they were still trying to control the narrative.

Tahrir: (Symbolic) Staging of a Movement

OLS: From the media reports here in Europe it seemed like Tharir was almost immediately becoming a central stage. Everything seemed to focus there...

ME: Then there was something that resonates with what you say. It's that it became an icon because it spread quite quickly and maybe too quickly, it was iconised. And I am not talking about the fact that it remains till now, a meeting place, but that it became a symbol for the media and the merchants, who were selling flags and so on, and who turned it into a souvenir shop in no time. You felt almost that it was a bit indecent, this iconisation which happened so fast. It was actually sometimes demeaning, we felt that it made what happened lose its meaning and power.[10]

In the beginning, due to its name which is 'Liberation Square', which is the proper translation, it was a convergence point. This was where all the marchers and the demos would converge.[11] And then it became a symbol because it was the stronghold of the uprising, and this was the space to protect. Of course, being a square with eight avenues going into it, we said we had to close ourselves inside it; it's like closing yourself into a trap so it made us very vulnerable. But because we were very vulnerable, it meant that we had to be very determined so either we won or we lost forever. And this really accentuated the determination of everyone, the way it was, the topography of the square.

Control and Confusion

They were controlling a narrative. Like, 'something very tiny happened, thank God! Three days later everybody has gone and see, we are cleaning up the square with our brooms!' And they would publish pictures of the square

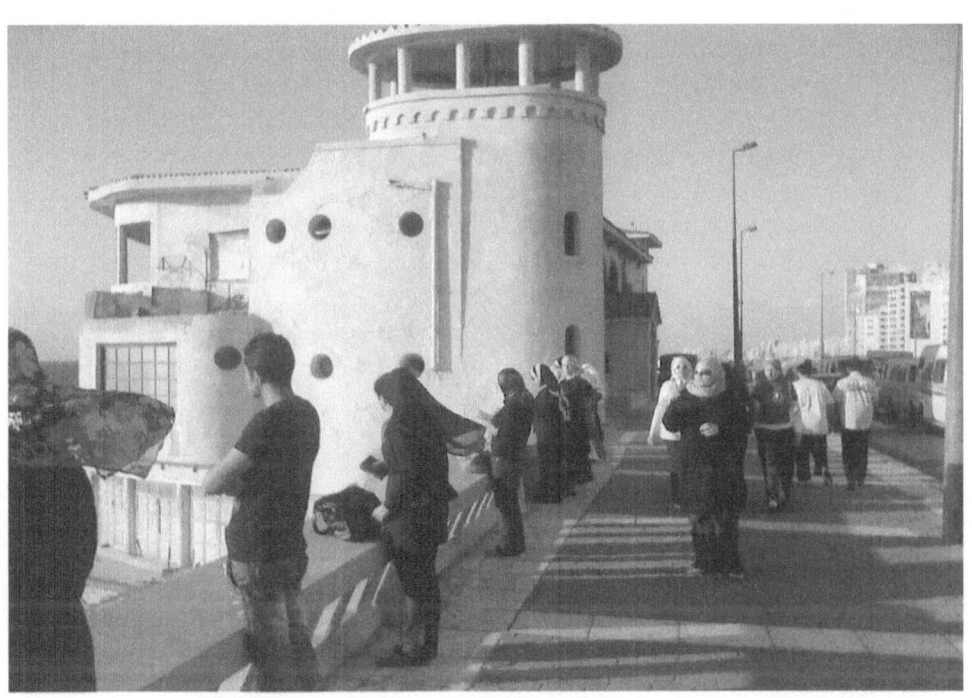

Small bands of people on Stanley Bridge in Alexandria 'wearing black clothes and looking deeply into the sea, contemplating, or reading Qur'an. No one seemed to really know what's going on. They were just there. I guess that was the original purpose of the "rally".'
Photo by Ehab El Badry, Mahalla, 14 April, 2008

that would show it empty in the official newspapers, whereas it would actually be filled with hundreds of thousands of people – the lies were huge! Because they know perfectly well that they have this type of control over the population because they have the privilege of the radio, television and four huge newspapers and they can very easily cast doubt on the rest and even say these people are manipulated by Mossad. They would actually add very contradictory theories that they were manipulated by Mossad, that they were also manipulated by Iran, that they were populated by the United States; I mean completely conflicting interests just to cast a total doubt on what's going on and it works.

Then, the Supreme Council of Armed Forces (SCAF) launched a smear campaign where 'Tahrir people' was a synonym of those agitated marginal people who are, you know, like thugs. They were basically turning the thing completely around and doing a smear campaign against activists, against citizens claiming their rights. Because after the revolution happened everybody had high hopes which dropped, one after the other. And today we are in a situation where we all realise there has actually been no progress and in fact a lot of regression in terms of freedom of expression, quality of life, that the economy is on its knees, and so and so and so, and no justice.[12]

You have 12 thousand Egyptians who will have been court-martialed, who are civilians and with hardly any trial, no legal representation or anything. So again, the people who are paying the price are trying to find channels of visibility and pressure. But we are finding ourselves again in this situation where everyone is saying how wonderfully Egypt has done in their revolution and is again collaborating with SCAF, shaking the hands of criminals, which is just killing us.

Media Battles

OLS: Just to be clear about what you've just said – would you say that the number one strategic mistake of the movement was not to take over the media infrastructure?

ME: Major – for me it's a major error.

OLS: Was there any discussion about that – any awareness? After these clashes would people debate the obvious alternatives of either building their own autonomous media structures to bypass traditional media or

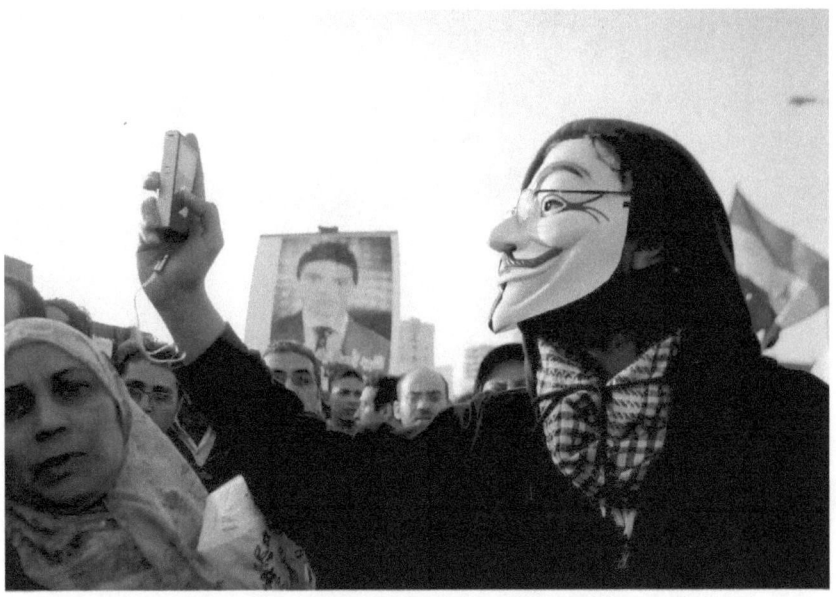

Participants shooting video during Funeral Procession in Tahrir.
Photo by Lilian Wagdy, Cairo, 2 December, 2011

transforming them? Was there any kind of reflexive discussion of the movement and of how to proceed with it?

ME: I don't believe so, otherwise they would have a plan. The thing is that you had tanks everywhere that were actually guarding the passageway around Maspiro, which is the central television building. The attitude here was completely different. I don't know, you might have heard of this tragedy that happened on 9 October where protesters gathered around Maspiro? It was a Coptic demonstration, they were all gathered after the church had been burnt down and they were demanding the fall of the Supreme Council of Armed Forces, and that this power be transferred to civilians and that we stop the military trials of civilians.

So they were putting on the pressure around this building, and on that day the military simply crushed the crowd by sending in armoured personnel carriers which ran around the crowd killing 28 people and injuring 1000. So this just means that as soon as there was something that they sensed would turn into a threat against Maspiro then they responded with extreme harshness. That just shows you how little risk they will take over that.[13]

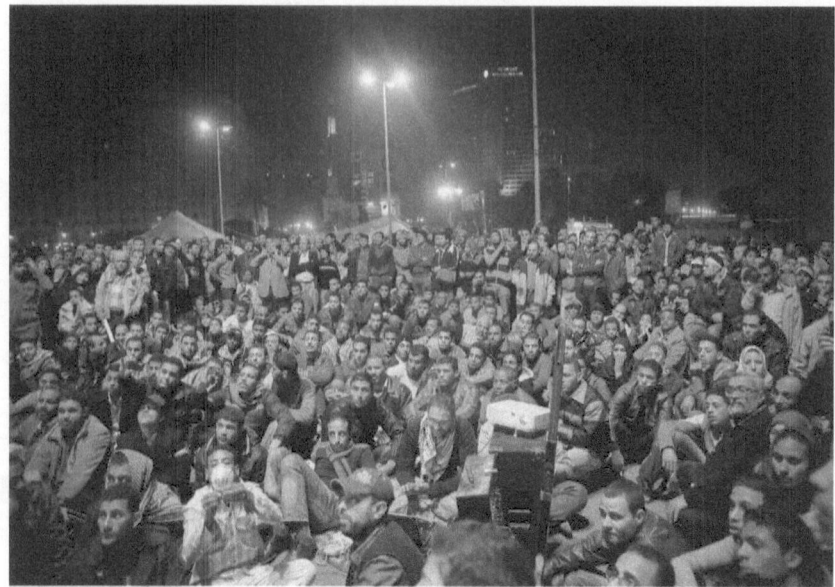

Activists in Tahrir Square on Friday night set up a projector to screen videos of the army's attacks on protesters during the previous week.
Photo by Hossam el-Hamalawy, Cairo, 23 December 2011

What happened was that when the uprising happened, we did not liberate the media. There is one building, the Television and National Radio building; in retrospect we should have occupied it and made sure it was completely cleaned up, and not returned to the surveillance and authority of the military which is guarding it like Fort Knox because, if they don't have access to this body, they can't operate because they only operate on lies, on distortions, on this information, dis-information. This is the stronghold of power – media.

The Counter-Revolution is Televised

OLS: What were the consequences of this mistake?

ME: So what we have to do now is respond to this flow of lies, of distortion, of propaganda, smear campaigns and so on by finding, actually developing again strategies or events, public reunions, so that the messages we send are not so often flooded by the response of the, let us call it, counter revolution.

And you see, the counter revolution is really televised, outrageously televised. And it is achieving horrible results, because it is so efficient. It divided the population, that means today and nine months after the revolution, anyone you ask about this swindle would tell you: 'What is this thing, this revolution? It was better before. Look around you, nothing is working.' All our hopes went down the drain.

It is interesting to remember that in the beginning of the Egyptian uprising, for six whole days, we had no internet and no telephone, no SMS and the movement only became bigger, maybe to some extent because of that. Because people had to leave home, they couldn't call each other so they had to meet each other and I am sure that it actually played a role in increasing the mobilisation, rather than frightening people, which is what the government wanted. And so, this showed us that everything went perfectly well with no cell phones, no internet, no Twitter, no nothing. It puts things into proportion.

So it's interesting to have this very privileged, unusual moment of six days without anything and everything is going perfectly well, everyone is communicating perfectly well, you know. And this just made me realise! I don't know if society in general is conducive, or maybe it is Egyptian society in general that is so conducive. But information flew. You could see it flying in Tahrir as well. It's another type of microcosm, it spread out. When you had information here, you also had it there just as you walked. You don't know how it works but it spreads, and so this was an interesting relationship of seeing how reality works, how virtuality works and you wonder which is faster.

Old Media Revisited: Writings on the Wall

Well if you go to Cairo right now, you can hardly find a wall that hasn't been covered with graffiti; there was an explosion of graffiti. And, there is something quite strange in Egypt; it's that walls aren't necessarily considered as special, except certain walls that would be under surveillance. But it is very common to see things written on the walls and nobody cares. People put their telephone numbers there, saying 'I give private lessons'. They make big stencils, or they paint the entire wall. The relationship to walls is a bit different. So what has changed now is the nature of the message, they are all political. You have some that represent Mubarak, the Field Marshall Tantawi, the strongman now in power, other figures, messages, Khaled Saeed, icons and symbols all over the place. They are often very primitive sentences, written with spray, which sometimes have even more power than a slick graphic artwork.[14]

OLS: So, what is your take on the role of 'new/social media' after all these experiences?

ME: I'm really going to state a generality right now but this type of tool really just empowers you to create your own impact and dissemination if you are willing to spend the time. So it's really like do-it-yourself media, do-it-yourself campaign, do-it-yourself impact, do-it-yourself reputation as well. There is no intermediary between you and a potentially very wide public. So I think this is what the internet brings – it widens your scope. You can play with these tools and actually if your content is timely and good and interesting to people and so on, it can with no intermediary and no budget and no anything, get out there, and this is good to know. You feel that if everything falls apart, you can still do this.

DIY Universalism

OLS: What is the overall significance of the Egypt experience in a wider, global context, in your view?

ME: I remember, and I am not the only one, that during those 18 days of the uprising up to the fall of Mubarak, we were extremely aware that it was not all about us. We experienced the universality of what was going on. There was something extremely human, that had nothing to do with our origin, our colour, our religion; we were just human and we were given to experience what humanity had when it was at its best. It is actually a very strong and rather overwhelming feeling and we saw that this was possible. It was like being given a peek of paradise – and then it closes again. And so it had nothing to do with being Egyptian, and we were very conscious that it could inspire or it could actually be; you'd wish for everybody to have access to the same experience.

And of course we are struggling to get a little bit of that back on a less utopian level with the institutions, to create a political life which is normal. We all had the feeling that it would export, it would travel around the world and that maybe in all of the countries where there is a separation or divorce

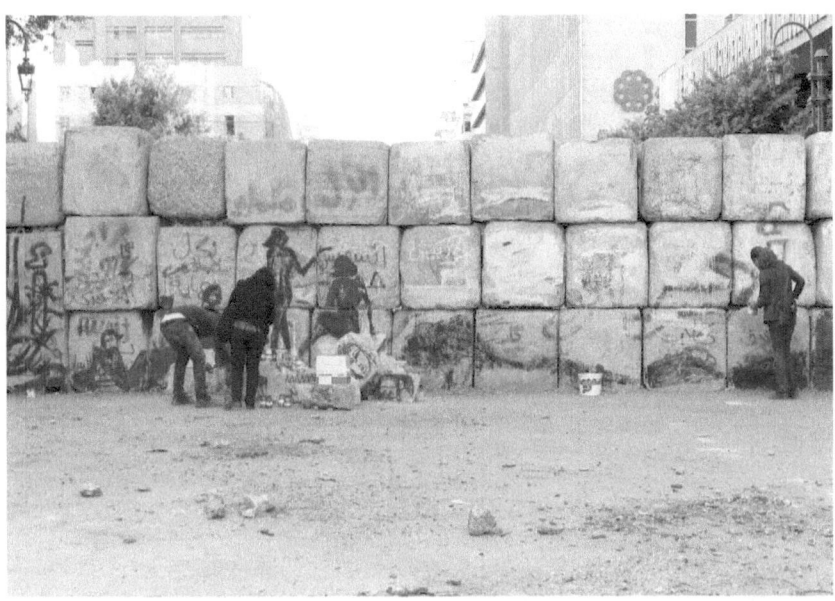

No Walls Graffiti, applied on street blockades erected by SCAF around Tahrir.
Photo by Gigi Ibrahim, Cairo, 9 March 2013

between the governments and the governed, that things would go in the same direction with the same kind of aspiration.

We have the support of people to people – we are talking about citizens and citizens – and this expresses itself through wilful collaboration. Like now for example with the Occupy movement which is in touch with people in Egypt and it's also in touch with people in Greece and so on.[15] In this community of interest it is easy to bring people together. We share knowledge, we share content, we make solidarity, we can actually expand the impact of an issue and raise international attention.

Free Space! Occupy and the Globalisation of a Performative Act

ME: During the revolution itself there was something quite strange; it wasn't a form of rejection, it just happened to be that way. We really weren't counting on anyone, we knew this time it had to be us. What's interesting to look at for me is how the Occupy movement comes right after, chronologically, and it's called 'occupy' which is in itself is a plan. 'Occupy' is already an action verb and so when people ask 'what are their demands?' - their demand is to occupy! This is the first demand and it's achieved. And what are they occupying? The public space, the public sphere and a place to gather, to talk. And actually, it is the quest for free space and this I find is the most common to all the Occupy movements. It's also true in Spain, in France in Europe and so on. It is telling us that space has been privatised and that we actually have to go fight for it, to get some back! Because we are so much on the internet and not talking to each other, we don't have free space to interact in. Meaning not a café or a Mall – but a free and open space. Something open which has no political colour, commercial colour, no colour at all. Something where I can just interact and exchange. So, I am very much against the bashing of all these movements which are described as a bunch of hippies with their music and guitars, singing songs and sitting together. That's fabulous I think.

Footnotes

1   http://manaala.net – Currently, February 2014, there is only a mirrored version online, provided via CloudFlare-backup.
2   What was true in November 2011, sadly was true end of 2013 and is still true in the beginning of 2014. In November 2013, Alaa was arrested again for allegedly encouraging a demonstration against the new constitution outside the Egyptian Parliament. He is currently in prison.
3   For an account on this early genealogy of political social media see an interview with Aalam Wassef, conducted by Howard Rheingold in 2011, http://storify.com/hrheingold/aalam-wassef-on-social-media-in-egypt-revolution
4   This risk was and is closely related to net-surveillance technologies provided by western companies (aided by export policies) like the infamous Finfisher software, that was also found in Egypt – see e.g., http://www.bloomberg.com/news/2012-07-25/cyber-attacks-on-activists-traced-to-finfisher-spyware-of-gamma.html
5   See FN #1.
6   See 'We all are Khaled Said' website, especially the section on 'Silent Stands': http://www.elshaheeed.co.uk/silent-stands/
7   For a deeper analysis see 'The Mahalla Strikes', chapter in The Prince and the Pharao by Brecht De Smet: https://www.academia.edu/2094331/CHAPTER_14_THE_MAHALLA_STRIKES_-_The_Prince_and_the_Pharaoh._The_Collaborative_Project_of_Egyptian_Workers_and_Their_Intellectuals_in_the_Face_of_Revolution
8   See Hossam el-Hamalawy Wikipedia page, http://en.wikipedia.org/wiki/Hossam_el-Hamalawy, his blog, http://www.arabawy.org/, and in particular his photostream, https://www.flickr.com/people/elhamalawy/, which forms an integral part of his activism.

9   For a good snapshot of this media-borne 'infection' see: http://www.huffingtonpost.com/democracy-now/tunisians-topple-tyranny-_b_810412.html
10 See Aya Nasser, 'The Symbolism of Tahrir Square', 2011 http://english.dohainstitute.org/release/ccfc38f8-eae6-4542-9fb0-13dd6075ed7c; and for a more extended consideration of the iconicity and image flows of Tahrir: Walter Gunning, 'Toward a Cinema of Revolution: 18 Days in Tahrir Square', 2011, http://www.politicalperspectives.org.uk/wp-content/uploads/Gunning-Tahrir-1.pdf
11 On the role of collective projections taking place on Tahrir, and the so-called 'Tahrir Cinema' by Mosireen see 'The Cairo Case' by Azin Feizabadi and Kaya Bekhalam, a presentation given during Video Vortex #9: http://tinyurl.com/tahrir-mosireen
12 On the economic part of subjugation, see the perspective of Ayoub Massoudi, former advisor of the Tunisian president Moncef Marzouki, titled 'From Tunisia to Egypt: The Great Confiscation', http://www.huffingtonpost.com/ayoub-massoudi/from-tunisia-to-egypt-the_b_3670356.html
13 For a detailed reconstruction of the Maspiro events see 'Maspero massacre underscores Egypt's unfinished revolution', http://storyful.com/stories/1000009424. See also 'The Cairo massacre and how to invent "religious conflicts"', http://www.antropologi.info/blog/anthropology/2011/cairo-clashes
14 See, Mia Gröndahl, *Revolution Graffiti: Street Art of the New Egypt*, American University in Cairo Press, 2012; and Sherif Boraïe (ed.), *Wall Talk – Graffiti of the Egyptian Revolution*, Zeitouna, 2012. In a broader context see also, Samia Mehrez (ed.), *Translating Egypt's Revolution: The Language of Tahrir*, The American University in Cairo Press, 2012.
15 See, 'To the Occupy movement – the occupiers of Tahrir Square are with you', http://www.theguardian.com/commentisfree/2011/oct/25/occupy-movement-tahrir-square-cairo; and 'Endorsement of a Solidarity Action and Letter for Egypt on Saturday, November 12th', http://occupyoakland.org/2011/11/egyptian-revolution-sat-4p/; as well as 'Solidarity Letter from Berlin', http://www.occupymedia.org/?page_id=657

PROCESS PROCESSED

JOSEPHINE BERRY SLATER

Immunisation, in defending against that which threatens, in saying no, takes into itself the 'no' which then becomes part of itself.

Marcel Duchamp has said: 'I believe that art is the only form of activity in which man, as man, shows himself to be a true individual who is capable of going beyond the animal state. Art is an outlet towards regions which are not ruled by time and space. To live is to believe, that's my belief.'[1] From this we can then say: art is an immunisation against man's 'animal state', and an activity that demarcates the boundary between *zoe* and *bios*, voice and language, by which humans (problematically) come to define themselves as human.

The threat of the animal state could be understood as a threatened indistinction between the self and the outside, of an assimilation into the common, and ultimately one of annihilation and death drive. As Roberto Esposito has pointed out, *immunitas* and *communitas* share a common root – *munus*, meaning 'gift' but also 'service'.[2] Immunity defends against our open-ended exposure to the violence implicit in the common, but also its open-ended demands and obligations, protecting its bearer from risky contact through an imposition of boundaries. Modernity's creation of the individual, then, is an immunisation against the threat of the common – based ultimately in our mutual exposure to being killed, in life – which is in turn sublated into the sovereign dispositif. To quote Esposito: 'In this sense sovereignty is the not being in common [...] of individuals, the political form of their desocialization.'[3] Esposito concludes that this substitution of individualised models for communitarian ones bears a structural connection with the process of modernisation.

If immunisation provides a hinge between life and politics, *zoe* and *bios*, how can we relate art's defence against 'the animal state' to this? It is a big question. But passing with reckless speed over large tranches of art history, let's move to its discovery of itself as its own ends, and the crisis of boundaries that this brings with it.

'Art for art's sake' is the moment in the mid-19th century when art relieved itself of its moral, didactic and utilitarian pretexts. In doing so, it declared itself to be its own end, and its own means. In this sense, it attempted to immunise itself from social use, in order to commit wholly to its own cause – which must by definition remain undefined, because it only finds definition through its own self-actualisation.

Art for art's sake, one might say, is a response to the procedures of the Enlightenment and the 'philosophy of doubt' that propelled them – as well as the social and political upheavals and reorderings of capitalist modernity.

The self-evident correspondence between phenomenal experience and reality, thought and being, was severed, as the techniques and equipment for the independent verification of universal truths autonomised from subjects, turning them, at best, into 'modest witnesses'. As the 'will to truth' reached its crisis in its radical decentering of the human, art's liberation from its job of naturalising cultural forms – its window dressing of relations of power – also precipitated a related trajectory of self-alienation. As Clement Greenberg conjectured in his 1961 essay 'Avant-garde and Kitsch', if following Aristotle, art had been understood as the imitation of nature, then avant-garde art's revolt is to develop by means of an 'imitation of imitating'.[4] Through this, art not only reveals its own development as one of contingency and process, but comes to elevate the processual and contingent as key to its methodology.

In this sense art, by imitating – and thus denaturalising – its own processes of imitation, also begins to imitate the discoveries of scientific rationalism and the life sciences. For Hannah Arendt, writing a few years earlier than Greenberg in the 1950s, the philosophy of doubt combines with the discovery, in the life sciences, of nature's eternal processual development to effect a simultaneous demotion of the built world, of fabricated things and generalised 'world alienation', in which there is no stable identity or place for humans.[5] The radical shattering of naturalism in culture, politics and society, is mourned in Arendt's writing as a loss of 'world' – defined as the home carved out by man within nature – which is swallowed up in the 'modern principle of process'.[6]

The swallowing up of 'world' by the processes unleashed by the Enlightenment's dialectic – whose ultimate threat is extinction – also brings with it the discovery of life as the 'highest good'.[7] In other words, life's drive to protect itself through the artifice of *ratio*, leads back by way of this threat to the discovery that, through life, man remains related to all other living organisms. *Zoe* erupts at the heart of all systems, and through this becomes the target of politics, economics and culture in the era of biopolitics.

In taking us beyond the 'animal state' art eventually leads, through the embrace of means without ends, and a fascination with process, to the ambiguous vindication of life – the same destination as modern politics. For the conceptual line that develops out of dada and Duchamp's related discovery of the readymade, this resolves into a distrust of the image whose conventions as well as its innovations are disparaged as matters of 'taste'.[8] Perhaps counterintuitively, the vindication of life entails, in this genealogical branch, the elevation of thought by which artists can defend against repetition and the iterations of style which produce the differential

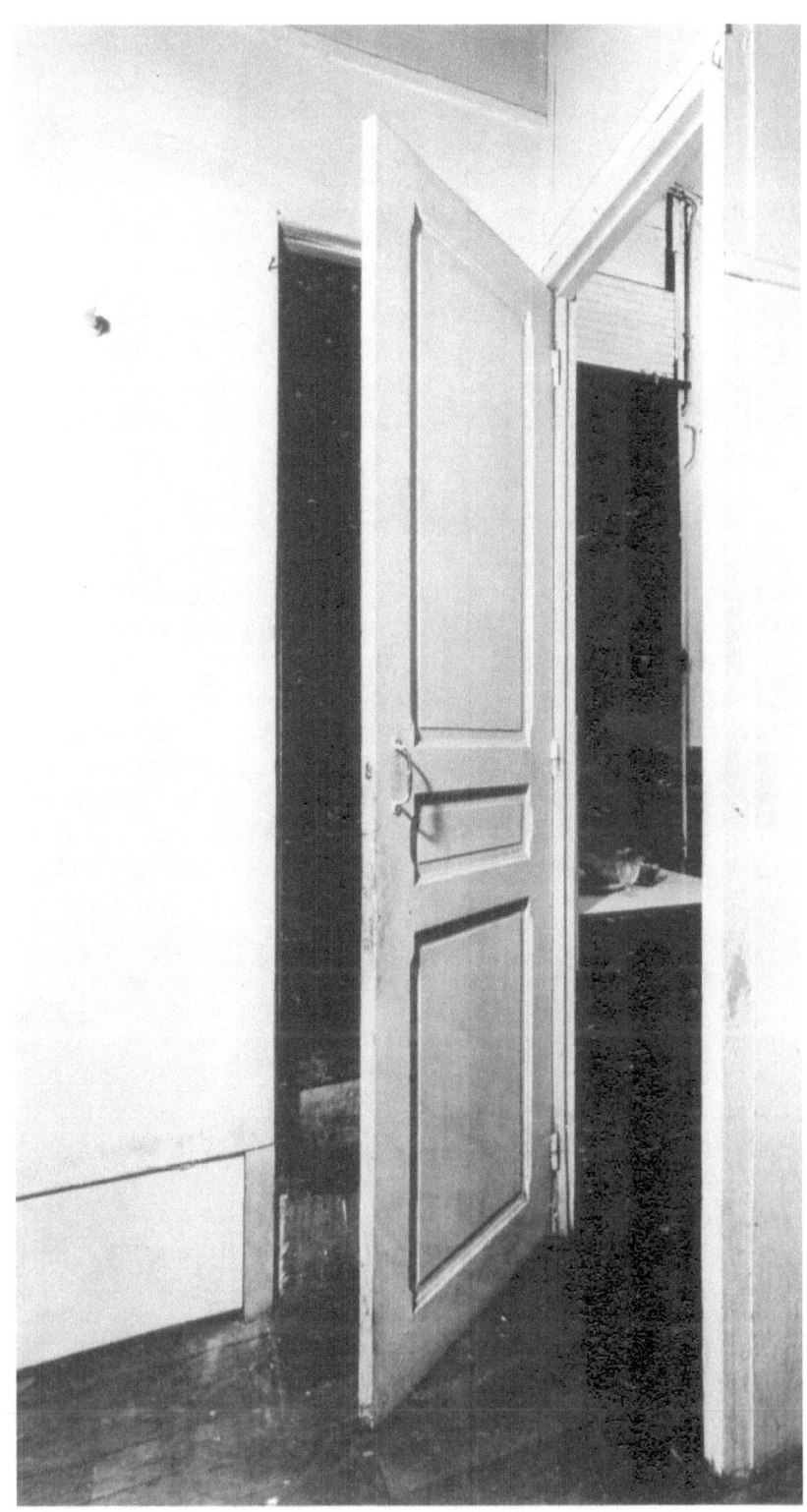

Marcel Duchamp, *Door, 11 Rue Larrey*, 1927

field of taste, that aider and abetter of social conventions and stasis. Through nomination's inflation of thought, all of being is imaginatively subjected to art's procedures. To state it briefly, becoming can itself become a readymade, or, according to Duchamp's instructions:

> by planning for a moment to come (on such a day, such a date such a minute), 'to inscribe a readymade' – The readymade can later be looked for. – (with all kinds of delays.) The important thing then is just this matter of timing, this snapshot effect, like a speech delivered on no matter what occasion but at such and such an hour. It is a kind of rendezvous.[9]

This is reminiscent of Nietzsche's 'eternal return' whereby all of becoming affirms itself in each transient moment. Duchamp looks for a way for life to affect itself, not through its figurative representation, but by the creation of a rendezvous with itself in the future in which it can experience its own desire for itself. For Agamben, the desire to persist in being is what we desire in the other, and what gives rise to love.[10] The art of the disenchanted anthropocene can at the same time be one of profound enchantment.

If the production of the individual is a structure of modernity by which assimilation into the common is deflected, then the desire to blur art and life is art's own defence against this form of desocialisation. In art's opening up to all of life through the conceptual mediation of nomination, it reveals the desire to break the immunological hold of modernity, and be reunited with an unspecified common. Not coincidentally, the appearance of the naked and sexualised body is also a significant chapter in this opening up of the artwork to the inclusions of its structural exclusions – one which often looked to see the cogito unhorsed by the powers of the libido.

But this tendency seemed to hit a limit in the 1960s with the affirmative vitalism of 'the happening' and various scripted encounters between art and its outside. Ciphers for becoming, such as spontaneity, participation and co-creation, were often merely self-confirming experiments which all too rarely pierced the limits of their own preconditions. The presumption of a Gaia-like good will, of a social and natural world which could be restored to some notional equilibrium, ended with the demise of the post-war economic boom and the oil/profits crisis of the 1970s. Process and common exposure took on a darker valence, in the image of resource exhaustion, capitalism's subsumption of struggles around social reproduction, and the disciplinary regulation of feedback – not to mention an explosion of sexually transmitted diseases.

Today, official culture immunises itself against the inflammatory potential of unscripted process, of singularising sequences, by processing process like spam. Antony Gormley's recent public sculpture, *One in Other*, in London's Trafalgar Square rotated participants as living sculpture on top of the fourth column on an hourly basis, after having thoroughly vetted them in advance. People took this as an opportunity to display exaggerated individualism or promote various charities and NGOs. In no case did this result in Rancière's definition of real participation, namely the invention of 'unpredictable subjects'. Here we see an enforcement of individualism conducted through the language and forms of openness. Participation has everywhere become a means to exclude through inclusion – the ultimate immunological procedure. Due to their shared aim of vindicating life, instrumental and governmental reason and aesthetic reason have cross-contaminated each other. Activity and its unleashing of new processes, of creating new beginnings, has a threefold implication: it is at once the target of biopower which wants to rule our self-activity; the ungovernable effect of thanatropic Enlightenment, and the imaginable means of escape from the desocialised suspension of modernity.

This text was presented as a talk given at The Matter of Contradiction: War Against the Sun symposium, March 2013, Limehouse Town Hall, http://lamatiere.tumblr.com/waragainstthesun

---

Footnotes

1   See, 'Marcel Duchamp. An Interview with James Johnson Sweeny', in James Nelson (Ed.), *Wisdom: Conversations with Elder Wise Men of Our Day*, New York: W.W. Norton & Company, 1958,
2   Roberto Esposito, *Bios: Biopolitics and Philosophy,* Minneapolis: University Of Minnesota Press, 2008.
3   Ibid.
4   Clement Greenberg, *'Avant-Garde and Kitsch', Art and Culture: Critical Essays,* (1961), Boston: Beacon Press, 1989.
5   Hannah Arendt, *The Human Condition*, Chicago: University of Chicago Press; Second Edition edition, 1998.
6   Ibid., p.308.
7   Ibid., p.319.
8   Duchamp, op. cit.
9   Marcel Duchamp, *The Writings of Marcel Duchamp*, Michel Sanouillet and Elmer Peterson (Eds.), New York: Oxford University Press, 1973, p.32.
10 Giorgio Agamben, *Profanations*, New York: Zone Books, 2007, p.58.

THE SUBSUMPTION OF SOCIALITY

As capitalism moves beyond the stage of 'formal subsumption' into that of 'real subsumption', capitalists are no longer content to encompass existing forms of production into the production of value, but must convert and transform all of life (production and reproduction) into capitalist forms, finding ways to extract value across all of social activity. Within this, our forms of relating, caring and of expression, of communicating and collaborating, are enclosed and templated. Networked media has played a determining though by no means exclusive role in such a transformation. As with forms of political struggle, expression and sociality are likewise defined by the conditions in which they arise, even when their objective is to challenge those same conditions.

This Lab phase proposes the practical and theoretical exploration of ways to (re)appropriate our own sociality, creativity, collaborative impulses and 'free labour' in the era of real subsumption. What pores or holes do media networks provide for us to develop alternative 'forms-of-life' within? What forms of sociality are mobilised by power and how are they mobilised? What forms of revolt or evacuation are open to the subject of human capital? How can we bend the tools of management and measure against themselves? Can creativity be freed from its industrial and governmental appropriations? How can 'care' escape circuits of expropriation? How are urban and other spaces that help to constitute our sociality being shaped? How can new forms of subject mapping, data-tracking, neo-Taylorisation, and logistical deployment be inverted, taken apart, perverted, used to create new collectivities? What would a truly 'communal' use of info-sharing and data gathering look like? And what should we make of the promise of 'open knowledge', 'open data', 'open access' and 'open source'?

NOTES ON SUBSUMPTION

ANTHONY ILES

The following is a set of introductory notes written for the Glossary of Subsumption event at Berlin's Public School in January 2013. During this event, co-hosted by Post-Media Lab, guests were invited to present, discuss and develop a glossary of terms relating to subsumption with a particular focus on recent developments in Information and Computation, Energy, Environment, Land and Physical Space, Health, Reproductive Labour, Education and Creativity.

For more information on the event, see: http://thepublicschool.org/a-glossary-of-subsumption/

Compiling these notes, I have drawn extensively on the work of Endnotes, in particular a text entitled 'The History of Subsumption'.[1]

Inherited from idealist philosophy (Schelling, Kant, Hegel) and used by Karl Marx to theorise the development of the capitalist mode of production, subsumption has emerged as an important term for contemporary theorists attempting to describe and periodise the development of technologies, knowledges and class relations under capital. These categories of human activity and society can be described as 'under capital' since 'subsumption' – which can be translated as submission, domination or subordination – describes a process by which the particular (concrete labour) is subsumed by a universal (value or capital's process of valorisation).

The shift from 'formal subsumption' to that of 'real subsumption' in our present moment is characterised by the profound separation of human needs from capitalist production, self-reproduction and expansion. Capital is no longer content to merely encompass existing forms of production in its pursuit of value, but must convert and transform all of life (production and reproduction) into capitalist forms. Through this ceaseless deterritorialisation, it finds ways to extract value across all forms of social, material and biological activity, radically altering them in its wake. Within this, our ways of relating, caring and of expression, of communicating and collaborating, are enclosed, templated and optimised. As ICT is folded into this process, the creation of new forms of sociality, new edges, speeds and channels of communicating, and an endless wake of data are produced by and for subjects. ICT accelerates capitalist subsumption but also changes the nature of struggle against it, forcing it, and us, into more bound and arguably intimate confrontations.

Jacques Camatte

An additional definition:

> Subsumption means rather more than just submission. *Subsumieren* really means 'to include in something', 'to subordinate', 'to implicate', so it seems that Marx wanted to indicate that capital makes its own substance out of labour, that capital incorporates labour inside itself and makes it into capital.[2]

Marx theorises subsumption as a two-stage process by which capital takes hold of an existing process (formal subsumption) and begins to shape and transform it to its own ends (real subsumption).

> If the production of absolute surplus-value was the material expression of the formal subsumption of labour under capital, then the production of relative surplus-value may be viewed as its real subsumption.'[3]

> In the case of an already existing labor process being subordinated to capital, Marx speaks of the formal subsumption of labor under capital. The sole difference from pre-capitalist conditions consists in the fact that the laborers work for a capitalist rather than for themselves. [...] If the labor process is transformed in order to increase productivity, Marx speaks of the real subsumption of labor under capital.[4]

Michael Heinrich stresses that by increasing the productivity of labour, which is only possible by transforming the production process itself, then the value of labour power and the value of the means of subsistence can be reduced. Even so, in this situation productivity can increase, real wages can decrease, more surplus value can be appropriated by the capitalist even while a rise in the living standards of the working class has been achieved. A greater portion of the working day now consists of surplus labour.[5]

Absolute and Relative Surplus-Value

> If the production of absolute surplus-value was the material expression of the formal subsumption of labour under capital, then the production of relative surplus-value may be viewed as its real subsumption.[6]

> The dynamic emanating from the production of relative surplus value [...] (accelerated technical development, a rising standard of living of the working class

simultaneous to rising profit) is subject, however, to a precondition not hitherto addressed: the majority of means of subsistence consumed in the working-class household have to be capitalistically produced.[7]

Heinrich indicates how this was only achieved in the 20th century. In particular Fordism illustrates the ability of capitalists to raise wages, change the consumption patterns of workers and (through constant technological improvements to the production process) see rising profits.[8]

> [..] real subsumption brings into play the reproduction of the proletariat. [...] Real subsumption establishes the systematic and historical interconnection between the reproduction of the proletariat and the the reproduction of capital.[9]

Théorie Communiste

Thus French group, Théorie Communiste, can say:

> The extraction of relative surplus-value affects all social combinations, from the labour process to the political forms of workers' representation, passing through the integration of the reproduction of labour-power in the cycle of capital, the role of the credit system, the constitution of a specifically capitalist world market [...], the subordination of science [...] Real subsumption is a transformation of society and not of the labor process alone.[10]

There are many other accounts and ways of periodising this shift in historical terms. Endnotes point out that those of Antonio Negri, Théorie Communiste (TC), Jacques Camatte, and we could add Carlo Vercellone and many others, converge on the period of the early 1970s, with each maintaining that this moment represents a fundamental shift. Yet, it cannot be that this corresponds to a beginning to real subsumption, since we would have to date that much earlier e.g. Fordism or even earlier e.g. Bourneville or numerous other examples in which capitalists attempted to model not only the production process but integrate health, education and leisure and subordinate it to the needs of production (Foxconn would indicate a parallel attempt to do this in the present).

For Negri the period after 1968 marks the 'end of the centrality of the factory working class as the site of the emergence of revolutionary subjectivity.' Through the 'total subsumption of society' capitalist production has become diffuse and encompasses all activity – a factory without walls or social factory. (Endnotes)

For TC a similar period indicates two distinct moments of massive capitalist restructuring:

> Phase 1 – 1913/18-1960s: Formal and real subsumption are characterised by self-affirmation of the proletariat.
> Phase 2 – 1968-1973-present: Capital as a social relation becomes more immediately internal and self-negation of the proletariat becomes the only possibility of revolution.

Carlo Vercellone

From similar tendencies discussed by Carlo Vercellone results a periodisation in which three principal stages of the capitalist division of labour and of the role of knowledge can be identified (even if these phases in part overlap with each other).

> The stage of formal subsumption develops between the beginning of the 16th and the end of the 18th century. It is based on the models of production of the putting-out system and of centralised manufacture. The relation of capital/labour is marked by the hegemony of the knowledge of craftsmen and of workers with a trade, and by the pre-eminence of the mechanisms of accumulation of a mercantile and financial type.

> The stage of real subsumption starts with the first industrial revolution. The division of labour is characterised by a process of polarisation of knowledge which is expressed in the parcelling out and disqualification of the labour of execution and in the over-qualification of a minoritarian component of labour power, destined to intellectual functions. The attempt to save time, founded on the law of value-labour, is accompanied by the reduction of complex labour into simple labour and by the incorporation of knowledge in fixed capital and in the organisation of the firm. The dynamic of capital accumulation is founded on the large factories (first of all, those of the Mancunian model, then those of Fordism), which are specialised in the production of mass, standardised goods.

> The third stage is that of cognitive capitalism. It begins with the social crisis of Fordism and of the Smithian division of labour. The relation of capital to labour

is marked by the hegemony of knowledges, by a diffuse intellectuality, and by the driving role of the production of knowledges by means of knowledges connected to the increasingly immaterial and cognitive character of labour. This new phase of the division of labour is accompanied by the crisis of the law of value-labour and by the strong return of mercantile and financial mechanisms of accumulation. The principal elements of this new configuration of capitalism and of the conflicts that derive from it are, in large measure, anticipated by Marx's notion of the general intellect.[11]

Temporality and Limits to Periodisation

At this point Endnotes make clear their differences with the above theorists:

> It is evident that, with the constant revolutionising of production that occurs in real subsumption, the world beyond the immediate process of production is itself dramatically transformed. The important qualification here, however, is that these transformations occur with — or as a result of — the real subsumption of the labour process under the valorisation process: they do not necessarily constitute an aspect of real subsumption itself; nor do they define it, and indeed they may actually be considered mere effects of real subsumption. [...] Nothing external to the immediate production process actually becomes capital nor, strictly speaking, is subsumed under capital.[12]

Endnotes deny subsumption as a linear historical process, secondly questioning the simplistic applicability to historical development of class relations at all.

> [...] according to Marx, though formal subsumption must precede real subsumption, real subsumption in one branch can also be the basis for further formal subsumption in other areas. If the categories of subsumption are applicable to history at all, this can therefore only be in a 'nonlinear' fashion: they cannot apply simplistically or unidirectionally to the historical development of the class relation.[13]

Marx himself described real subsumption as a revolution which is both 'complete' and 'constantly repeated' in the 'Results...'

Patrick Murray argues that the terms 'formal subsumption' and 'real subsumption' refer first to concepts of subsumption and only secondarily – if at all – to historical stages.

Surreal Subsumption or Surreal Domination

This playful term was developed by the occasionally London-based group Melancholic Troglodytes to characterise the present coexistence of formal and real subsumption and apparent return to prior forms of primitive accumulation (direct appropriation of wealth and resources by capital-in-formation):

> The Melancholic Troglodytes pick up on this dynamic, calling it 'surreal subsumption' – the co-existence of 'real subsumption' (a phase of capitalist development in which all of life becomes subject to exchange value) and 'primitive accumulation' (a stage in the transition to capitalism in which value is accumulated through theft or looting).[14]

> The surreal phase we have postulated will come to replace the real phase of capital domination. What is interesting about this emerging phase is that it consists of four methods of surplus value extraction thus giving both capital and labour more flexibility. The two common forms of surplus value extraction (formal and real) are now becoming sandwiched between two more, provisionally named the pre-formal and post-real methods of extraction.[15]

Itzván Mézáros

Mézáros calls real subsumption the 'advent of the second order of mediations' and identifies it with a specific, but unnamed period of human history. He stresses the total subordination of social reproductive functions and relates it to the separation and subordination of use value to exchange value (this is also an important theme for Vercellone). In this sense, limitations of (human) need do not constrain the reproductive expansion of capitalism.

> Capital, as such, is nothing but a dynamic, all-engulfing and dominating mode and means of reproductive mediation, articulated as a historically specific set of structures and institutionally embedded as well as safeguarded social practices. It is a clearly identifiable system of mediations which in its properly developed form strictly subordinates all social reproductive functions – from gender and family relations to material production and even to the creation of works of art – to the absolute requirement of capital expansion, i.e. of its own continued expansion and expanded reproduction as a system of social metabolic mediation.[16]

Conclusion*

In the transformation of production and reproduction into capitalist forms one can see that organising universities, childcare, hospitals along the lines of the capitalist labour process makes sense to capitalists desperately seeking profits from any available source. However, on the present model this round of accumulation may simply exhaust itself and deliver only rent rather than surplus value. There is a return to a despotic mode expanded, but this does not necessarily spell success for capital. Without falling into vitalism, how can we disaggregate what has been described as life, or the human from the entropic descent of capitalism? Moreover, should we? Against the negative returns of capitalist futures, there is not necessarily a need to set against them an affirmative force of life. Rather, could we consider what are the weak links in the chain of present social organisation and breaking them in the service of a movement of both negation and greater socialistion rather than a further decline?

Further Questions

There are still a number of questions of exactly what is meant by the concept of 'personification' and the 'runaway of capital' in the work of Jacques Camatte. He also attributes these related dynamics to a tendency described as the 'anthropomorphism of capital'. 'Personification' here could refer to the tendency for subjects to internalise capital's programme as their own and thus a shifting view of capital as directed through the state, to capital as directed by the aggregate activity of individuals or monads. The runaway of capital can be understood through the related term, 'autonomisation', by which capital internally separates elements of the production process. On an expanded scale the reproduction of capital becomes increasingly independent from the reproduction of labour-power and this could be related to forms of financialisation, by which circulating capital self-augments, apparently without passing through production and surplus-value extraction. However, this view could also be challenged by considering in more precise detail the mediations by which finance capital restructures production and investments in its interests. Itzván Mézáros also discusses a 'personification' of both capital and labour, by which we can understand the labourer / concrete labour as a mere function of capital – an automatic subject responding to the particular dynamics of capital.

Alienation, as a term is closely related to subsumption and tends to be approached in a very loose way in contemporary debates. The alienation of the worker in production occurs in both a definitive and piecemeal fashion:

> Since machinery is continually seizing on new fields of production, its 'temporary' effect is really permanent. Hence the character of independence from and estrangement towards the worker, which the capitalist mode of production gives to the conditions of labour and the product of labour, develops into a complete and total antagonism with the advent of machinery.[17]

Marx is clear that the introduction of machinery enacts a reversal of practical power relations in production:

> In handicrafts and manufacture, the workman makes use of a tool, in the factory, the machine makes use of him. There the movements of the instrument of labour proceed from him, here it is the movements of the machine that he must follow.[18]

This reversal has henceforth become the ontological foundation of the ongoing relationship between capital and labour – capital's perspective, becomes the real material relationship between capital and labour.

> Machinery is put to a wrong use, with the object of transforming the workman, from his very childhood, into a part of a detail-machine. In this way, not only are the expenses of his reproduction considerably lessened, but at the same time his helpless dependence upon the factory as a whole, and therefore upon the capitalist, is rendered complete.[19]

However, this account is in contradiction with the widespread contemporary use of the term 'alienation', by which it is further psychologised. So, the question is: are we any more or less alienated now than when capital first began rendering (through machines) our products and capacities for social labour as alien? Is it not that we are only ever further away from the moment when this dynamic was rendered 'complete'? Is the question how to reverse the process, or how to depart from this situation? Moreover, what is the situation of sociality under these terms and framework. Is sociality counted by capital, or simply counted as free? And this remains the questionable strength of subsumption as a perspective, if real subsumption includes the reproduction of the worker into capital's reorganisation of production which in turn re-shapes the social field tout court, can life and capitalist life be meaningfully separated?

*This section of the notes was updated for a talk at a workshop on subsumption, The Theory and Politics of Subsumption held at Birkbeck University, London 25 May 2013, 12-6pm

---

Resources

Further sections on subsumption by Marx can be found throughout *Vols. 30-34 of Marx and Engels Collected Works* (esp. Vol. 30, pp.54-348; Vol 33, pp. 372-387; Vol.34, pp.93-121).

Chris Arthur, 'The Possessive Spirit of Capital: Subsumption/Inversion/Contradiction', *Re-reading Marx: New Perspectives after the Critical Edition*, Riccardo Bellofiore and Roberto Fineschi (eds.), UK: Palgrave, 2009.

Jacques Camatte, *Capital and Community: the results of the immediate process of production and the economic work of Marx*, David Brown (trans.), http://www.marxists.org/archive/camatte/capcom/

Enrique Dussel, *Towards an Unknown Marx: A Commentary on the Manuscripts of 1861-63*, Yolanda Angulo (trans.), London: Routledge, 2001, http://libcom.org/library/towards-unknown-marx-commentary-manuscripts-1861-63

Endnotes, 'A History of Subsumption', *Endnotes II*, http://endnotes.org.uk/articles/6

Andres Saenz De Sicilia, Time and Subsumption, May 2013
http://reificationofpersonsandpersonificationofthings.files.wordpress.com/2013/07/time-and-subsumption-andres.pdf

Karl Marx, *1861-63 Manuscripts*, MECW Volumes 30 and 33, http://www.marxists.org/archive/marx/works/1861/economic/index.htm

Karl Marx, *The Process of Production of Capital, Draft Chapter 6 of Capital: Results of the Direct Production Process*, Ben Fowkes (trans.), 1864, http://www.marxists.org/archive/marx/works/1864/economic/

Patrick Murray, 'The Social and Material Transformation of Production: Formal and Real Subsumption in Capital, Volume I', *The Constitution of Capital: Essays on Volume I of Marx's Capital*, Riccardo Bellofiore and Nicola Taylor (Eds.), UK: Palgrave, 2004.

Massimiliano Tomba, 'Historical Temporalities of Capital: An Anti-Historicist Perspective', *Historical Materialism*, 2009, Vol. 17, no. 4, pp.44-65.

Anthony Iles, 'Notes on Subsumption', http://saladofpearls.wordpress.com/2013/12/22/notes-on-subsumption/

Carlo Vercellone, 'From Formal Subsumption to General Intellect: Elements for a Marxist Reading of the Thesis of Cognitive Capitalism', 2007, http://hal.inria.fr/docs/00/26/36/61/PDF/historicalpubliepdf.pdf

---

Footnotes

1. Endnotes, 'A History of Subsumption', *Endnotes* #II, http://endnotes.org.uk/articles/6
2. Jacques Camatte, 'Capital and Community', http://www.marxists.org/archive/camatte/capcom/
3. Karl Marx, 'Results of the Direct Production Process', (MECW 34), p.429.
4. Michael Heinrich, *An Introduction to the Three Volumes of Karl Marx's Capital*, 2012, Monthly Review Press, pp.118-119.
5. Ibid., p.120.
6. Karl Marx, 'Results of the Direct Production Process' (MECW 34), p.429.
7. Michael Heinrich, op. cit., p.121.
8. Ibid., p.121.
9. Endnotes, op.cit., p.145.
10. Théorie Communiste quoted in ibid., p.145.
11. Carlo Vercellone, 'From Formal Subsumption to General Intellect: Elements for a Marxist Reading of the Thesis of Cognitive Capitalism', *Historical Materialism* 15 (2007) 13-36.
12. Endnotes, op.cit., pp.148-149.
13. Endnotes, ibid., pp.148-149.
14. Josephine Berry Slater, *Proud To Be Flesh*, New York: Autonomedia, 2008.
15. Melancholic Troglodytes, 'Disrespecting Multifundamentalism', in ibid.
16. Itzván Mézáros quoted in Ricardo Antunes, *The Meanings of Work*, Leiden/Boston: Brill, 2012, p.7.
17. Karl Marx, *Capital* Vol.1, p.558.
18. Ibid., p.547.
19. Ibid., p.54

DESTRUCTIVE DESTRUCTION – AN ECOLOGICAL STUDY OF HIGH FREQUENCY TRADING

INIGO WILKINS & BOGDAN DRAGOS

What follows is an account of the concepts of information and noise as they apply to an analysis of high frequency trading according to 'heterodox economics'. This account will highlight the evolutionary path that has led to the present micro-structure of financial markets and allow for a diagnosis of the contemporary financial ecology. High Frequency Trading (HFT) is a subset of algorithmic trading which works at very low time horizons (100 milliseconds) and requires massive information processing capacities. Following recent developments such as flash crashes and various technical break-downs, it is crucial to unpack the black-box of algorithmic high-frequency trading in order to understand its potential impact on wider social and economic systems. This will entail the application of various scientific theories to the financial domain that extend classical models of reversible functions, and go beyond models based on efficiency and equilibrium, encompassing a much wider class of irreversible transformations.

According to heterodox economics the development of thermodynamics brought an end to the dominance of classical physics in economic theory, in particular the dogma of efficient markets hypothesis, and reversal to equilibrium. It is this significant theoretical upheaval that allows Nicholas Georgescu-Roegen to say that the law of entropy is the basis of the economy of life at all levels.[1] Writing in the turbulent '70's, amidst the oil crisis, it became apparent to him that classical economic theory could no longer be an adequate model in addressing the huge task of third world underdevelopment, depletion of natural resources, increasing pollution, overpopulation, etc. In his attempt to deal with these issues, he recognised that the main barrier in repositioning economic theory on new grounds was its reliance on Newtonian mechanics. As the Midnight Notes Collective argue, Enlightenment thought was concomitant with a drive to the extraction of absolute surplus value during the first wave of real subsumption in the industrial revolution.[2] Georgescu-Roegen advocated the replacement of this idealised paradigm with thermodynamics whose second law (that the entropy of an isolated system tends to a maximum) would offer a much more fruitful theoretical foundation for economics. It should be noted at this point that although economic theory is even now still dominated by reversible models based on the supposition of efficiency and equilibrium at the abstract level, in practical terms thermodynamics had already significantly altered the political economy through the 19th century preoccupation with exhaustion, leading to a 'science of work' that concretised in the Taylorisation of the work-force after WW1.

The true novelty of Georgescu-Roegen's formulation lies in his proposal for a fourth law of thermodynamics, where it is not only energy that is subject to decreasing returns, but also matter; 'friction robs us of available matter'.[3] He thus identifies an ultimate supply limit of low entropy matter-energy; a 'source of absolute scarcity' consisting of a terrestrial stock and a solar flow.[4] This should not be understood as a reductionist account capable of explaining the causal structure of everything, but rather the identification of an abstract functional schematic whose explanatory coherence may be supplemented or extended by further theoretical devices. In particular, although thermodynamics can help to describe the conditions of class struggle and the divergence between market valuation mechanisms and the actual value of resources, it cannot account for the lived experiences of the former, and offers no substantial critique of the latter. However, it does allow for the reinsertion of the economic process into much wider physical, chemical and biological processes. For if the entropy law operates at all levels, then one can understand the economic process as a continual exchange between low and high entropy, just as dissipative systems maintain coherence through the reduction of energy gradients. An energy gradient is a differential; such as that between hot and cold, or between disparate prices; whose value can be tapped through the application of work. This is a naturalised view of finance, however it must be clearly stated that such a naturalisation does not entail a valorisation of present economic conditions. Rather, the economy, like the environment, exhibits a high degree of structural and functional redundancy, such that a great number of contingent modes of organisation are possible. Lets be clear here, to say that something is natural is not to say that it is good, after all a tumour is natural. It is just to argue that it is subject to a materialist analysis, without claiming to exhaustively describe all its aspects. Moreover, we must not conflate biological and economic ecologies, but rather treat them in their specificity.

It is useful, at this point, to clarify the distinction between low and high entropy. For the purpose of elaborating an ecological economics, Georgescu-Roegen understands the economy as a process that transforms available free energy into unavailable bound energy, that is to say the exploitation of a gradient. The former may be understood both as specific concentrations of material-energetic structures, such as oil or gold, and the potentiality for value extraction offered by living labour; while the latter is exemplified by waste, pollution, highly diffuse forms of matter-energy such as heat, and those forms of dead labour that no longer afford value extraction.

The economic process is the modulation by which a certain dissipative system maintains itself by continually 'inputting' free energy and 'outputting' bound energy. This entails a local growth of efficiency, or increase in the throughput of energy, that evolves according to the maximum entropy principle (MaxEnt), where the entropy of the microstates that do not correspond to the successful application of a function or technology are maximised such that the energetic cost is minimised for a given utility.[5] This local reduction of entropy is 'observer dependent', however it also necessarily results in an increase in 'observer independent' entropy according to the maximum entropy production principle (MEPP).[6] Effectively this means that biological, technical and economic evolution all lead inevitably towards an amplification of entropy at the environmental level. Nevertheless there is a high degree of contingency that determines the rate of throughput.

Within the field of evolutionary economics the notions of energy and information gradients become essential in understanding the dynamics of socio-economic change. In this sense, a certain abstract evolutionary matrix is common to all open systems, whether physical, chemical, biological or socio-economic.

> If there is an energy gradient available, a simple dissipative structure will exploit it. Similarly, if there is an information/knowledge gradient available, a socio-economic structure will grow and develop around this continual process of reduction.[7]

Ever since Friedrich Hayek and Eugene Fama, information becomes a crucial vector in understanding financial markets. For Hayek, markets are a way of collecting and aggregating available information. Fama understood efficient markets as reacting instantly to new information, thereby unproblematically reflecting all available information. While we certainly do not agree with the wider premises and conclusions of these liberal economists, it is important to understand economic systems as collective calculating devices that compute transient equilibriums.[8] Balancing economic, computational and thermodynamic perspectives, markets may be defined as dissipative structures coping in an entropic/noisy environment by reducing both energetic and information gradients. This becomes particularly apparent in modern capitalist economies. The current swarm of financial actors, including human, non-human and hybrid systems, feed off a social production of knowledge and its informational friction. An evolutionary process of variation, coordination and selection, leads to differential levels of fitness and to huge asymmetries in terms of collecting and processing

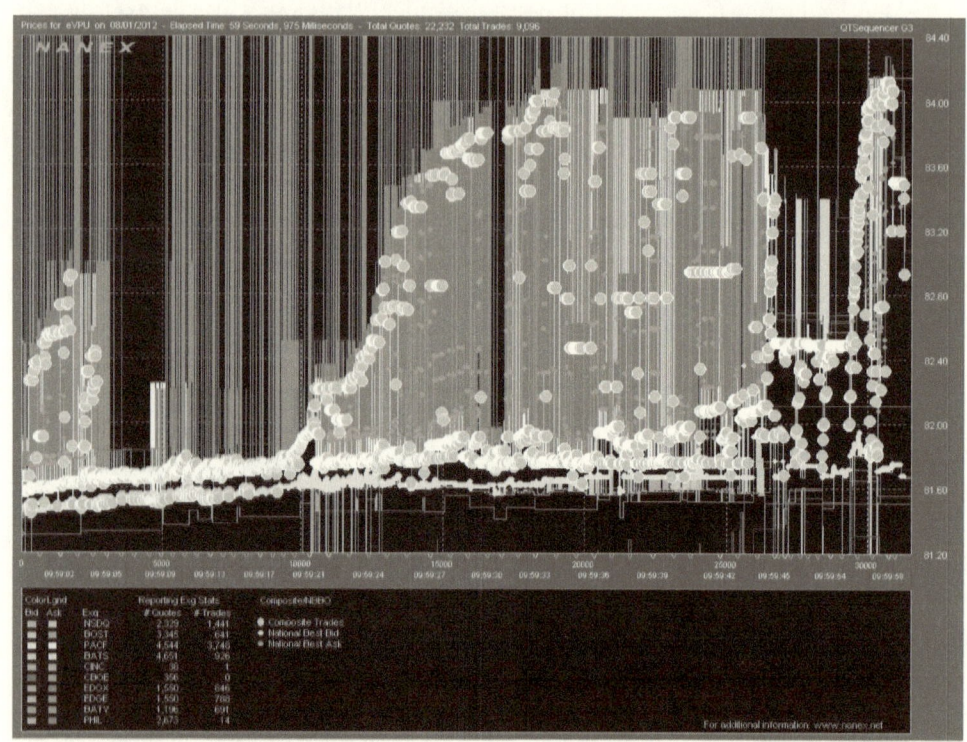

A Nanex chart from 08/01/12 showing the bid and the ask in one stock (a utilities ETF), and how at first the bid/ask are tight, but then just before 10.00 AM went totally wild.
Image Inigo Wilkins and Bodgdan Dragos

information, and hence to the creation of increasingly complex structures with higher rates of change. Such systems are characterised by non-linear risk situations featuring high interconnectivity and super-spreaders that amplify contagion.

In this sense, the main activity of finance is the bearing of uncertainty, but more precisely the reduction of an energetic and informatic gradient, fuelled by the ever-growing heterogeneity of the market.[9] Financial actors are not only an intermediary between producers and users of information, but they also 'assume a hermeneutic function' of performative interpretation, and moreover occupy the point of overlap between an information network and a liquidity network.[10] Maintaining itself at that particular juncture, allows the financial intermediary to access and reduce a very steep energy/information gradient. The investment bank therefore sits at the nexus of an informal information marketplace for price-relevant information.[11]

Our argument is that High Frequency Trades (HFTs) are complex sociotechnical systems that thrive both through the production of noise and by the reduction of information gradients, operating at a high rate of throughput and offsetting noise/entropy to the wider financial ecology. In order to explain these claims it is necessary to briefly chart the evolution of computing within finance and the subsequent appearance of algorithmic trading. From carrier pigeons and the transatlantic telegraph cable to contemporary ICT, finance has always been a site for intensive technical innovation. This is no surprise, inasmuch as financial actors thrive by accessing and reducing information gradients and exploiting communication inefficiencies.

More recently, the shift from open-outcry face-to-face trading to automated electronic trading has represented a huge leap in efficiency and the reduction of transaction costs. However, even Milton Friedman was aware that there is an 'intrinsic paradox built into the assumption of efficient markets', since efficiency is maintained by detection of inefficiencies, the closer to absolute efficiency the less inefficiencies can be discovered; so the market can never achieve absolute efficiency.[12] There is thus a complex dialectical interplay between drives to market efficiency and inefficiency. As the market approaches efficiency, there are less opportunities for arbitrage by informed traders (who gauge the discrepancy between the current price and the fundamental value of the underlying asset), and uninformed 'noise traders' progressively dominate the market.[13] This inevitably leads to the inflation of bubbles, with the subsequent collapse to fundamental values (when it is not brought on through market manipulation) occurring in an entirely unpredictable manner.

The market thus oscillates asymptotically around the attractor of zero information friction in an incomputably random orbit. While this movement receives its impetus from the dialectical, or apparently co-constitutive relation between efficiency and inefficiency, its trajectory and effects are far from reversible, resulting in the non-dialectical destruction of whole swathes of economic actors largely at the base of steep energy gradients.[14] Witness the wave of repossessions following the sub-prime mortgage crisis, or the assymetric distribution of debt organised by the austerity regime. A point made by Evan Calder Williams following Bordiga's description of capital as 'Murderer of the Dead.'[15]

Ever since the mid-'80s, there has been an incredible growth in the adoption of ICT and algorithms in the marketplace. From the computer terminals that were simply assisting human traders to the contemporary HFT software, we have seen the emergence of this new financial ecosystem, a highly complex computational matrix.[16] Algorithms are no longer tools, but they are active in analysing economic data, translating it into relevant information and producing trading orders.[17] This transition represents a new phase of real subsumption affecting all economic actors and social conditions. That is, if labour relations are reorganised around mechanics in the industrial revolution, then thermodynamics and cybernetics in the last two centuries, the current phase of real subsumption may be understood according to contemporary scientific transformations. This is often called the 'nano-bio-info-cogno revolution', and is based on distributed networks and 'friction free' systems (i.e. superconductors, ubiquitous computing). However, the importance of Georgescu-Roegen is his assertion that no such friction-free economy is possible, since the drive to efficiency is limited by the absolute scarcity of low entropy resources and met with a corresponding increase of exhaustion or resistance issuing from labour power.

Neil Johnson et al. identify a 'robot phase transition' after 2006 where the sub-millisecond speed and massive quantity of robot-robot interactions exceeds the capacity of human-robot interactions. They argue that operating at such timescales is intrinsically unstable and 'characterized by frequent black swan events with ultrafast durations'.[18] While Nassim Taleb's black swan theory is contentious, the conceptual core may be subtracted from his wider project, and refers to high-impact real contingencies as opposed to the structured randomness that casinos and quantum physics display. Analogous to the well-known effect in systems engineering where small cracks in a fuselage build up to a breaking threshold, financial friction is so high that micro-fractures in the form of mini flash-crashes proliferate, threatening the whole ecology.[19] Moreover, through the logic of encapsulated coding they employ, algorithmic trading software platforms are intrinsically open to abusive practices, and represent highly opaque and consequently 'unworkable interfaces'.[20]

In order to address the topic of HFT rigorously, we must not conflate the material specificities that define its heterogeneity; distinctions must be made between electronic, program and algorithmic trading, where HFT is a heterogeneous subset of all three.[21] 'The universe of computer algorithms is best understood as a complex ecology of highly specialized, highly diverse, and strongly interacting agents.'[22] Within this line of technical and financial innovations, we can see various types of trading strategies that employ an equally diverse population of market order types. Further, from an ecological perspective one can distinguish between various trading and execution algorithms, but also 'predatory' relationships. 'Strategies, markets and regulations co-evolve in competitive, symbiotic or predator-prey relationships as technology and the economy change in the background.'[23]

For example, pairs trading strategies (whose computational costs are so high they only took off after the '80's ICT revolution) unilaterally feed on the predictable price reversals engendered by portfolio balancing, just as short-term strategies prey on their long-term counterparts to the point of extinction.[24] Certain 'species' try to efficiently execute a trade, so as to achieve minimal market impact. They split large orders into smaller packs and execute them at certain time intervals. More evolved versions, like 'volume-weighted average price' (VWAP) algorithms, employ complex randomisation functions coupled with econometrics to optimise the size and execution times depending on overall trading volumes.[25] Moreover, new ecological niches have emerged in order to obfuscate the execution of large orders, known as 'dark pools'.[26] There are other types who try to profit from identifying and anticipating such trades, the algorithms sometimes referred to as 'predatory'.[27] Perhaps the best example of such a frequency-dependent evolutionary path, one that is well-known for its compulsive non-adaptive drive, is the proliferation of low-latency algorithms that profit from the transmission speed differentials inherent in the geography of the globally integrated financial system, and the material transformations these informatic relations entail.[28]

Such strategies of camouflage, mimesis and deception are endemic in predator-prey relationships, fuelling a run-away propagation of non-adaptive mutations according to the non-equilibrium dynamics of the 'Red Queen Effect', and are modelled in evolutionary game theory as crypsis.[29] In his discussion of the pathological tendencies of technological capitalism Ray Brassier cites Roger Callois' investigation of thanatropic mimicry, pointing out that such effects are irreducible to equilibrium models of dialectical resolution, and may often terminate in non-dialectical self-destruction.[30] 'In mimicking their own food,' Brassier writes, 'leaf insects such as the Phyllium frequently end up devouring each other'[31] He continues, some pages later:

> Enlightenment consummates mimetic reversibility by converting thinking into algorithmic compulsion: the inorganic miming of organic reason. Thus the artificialization of intelligence, the conversion of organic ends into technical means and vice versa, heralds the veritable realization of second nature [...] in the irremediable form wherein purposeless intelligence supplants all reasonable ends.[32]

Global finance can be seen as the staging ground for a continual redistribution of energy and information gradients; HFT is a prime example of this kind of evolutionary landscape. At a high enough level of liquidity, information friction and disparity allow for the emergence of computationally intensive systems that can effectively reduce gradients and extract rents.[33] While it is true that HFT accounts for a large part of market transactions, the profits are not the most significant among market participants. In the end, all of the 'bigger' actors tolerate low-latency trading firms because they provide much needed liquidity. Nevertheless, HFT exists because at certain volumes of trading, they enjoy a systematic advantage, which is the result of a 'technicality' of trading that is opaque to outsiders.[34] They manage to 'survive' by exploiting information gradients that 'slower' market participants are unable to access.

> Nanex: On ... Aug 5, 2011, we processed 1 trillion bytes of data ... This is insane. ... It is noise, subterfuge, manipulation. ... HFT is sucking the life blood out of the markets... [A]t the core, [HFT] is pure manipulation.[35]

Such reactions might seem dramatic, but they testify to the intense struggle going on in the computational matrix of finance every day. An ecological perspective emphasises the complex interdependencies between different financial 'species'. Every participant is constantly processing market noise in an attempt to reduce it as much as possible to relevant information. The subsequent decisions and market orders represent more noise for the other participants, that is to say, an irreversible output of high-entropy. As long

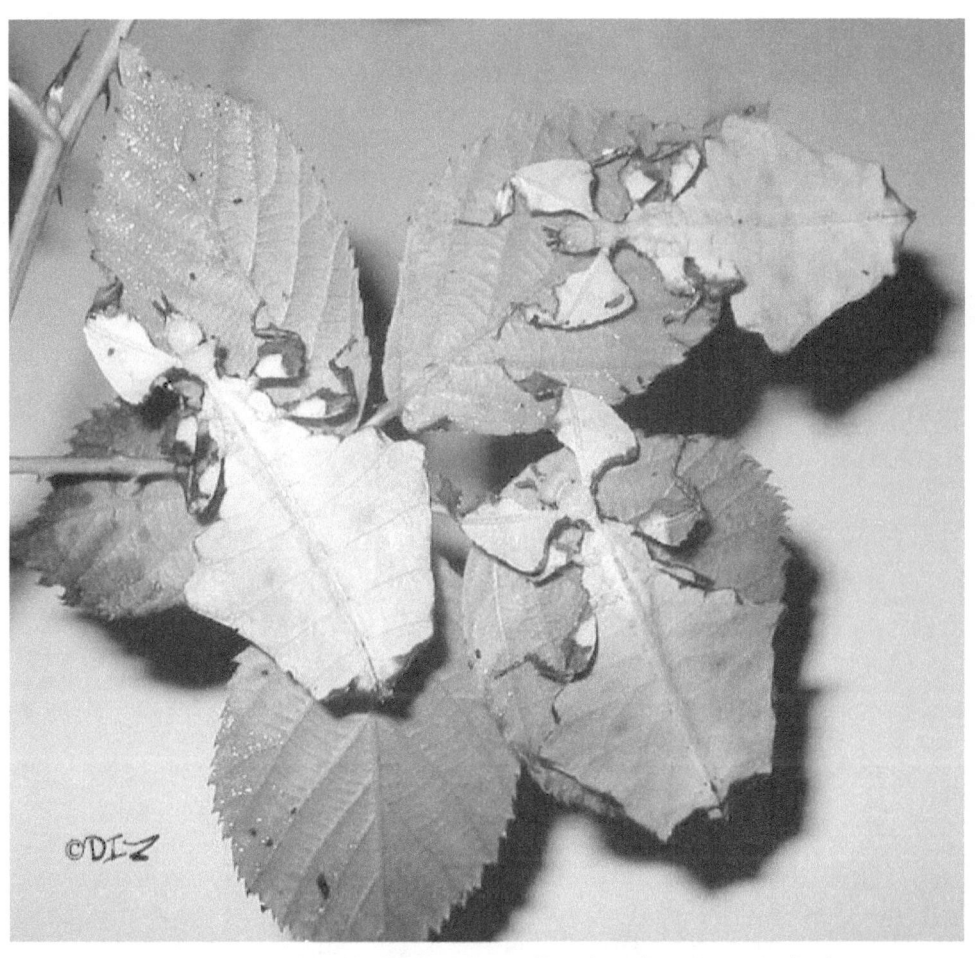
'Leaf insects such as the Phyllium frequently end up devouring each other'
Image Inigo Wilkins and Bodgdan Dragos

as there is enough disparity and enough heterogeneity in the market, high-frequency traders can profit from the underlying friction and produce more noise. It is precisely this persistent inefficiency of markets that informs heterodox economics.

> Because of bounded rationality, financial traders can't do everything at once – they tend to specialize. These specialized traders interact with one another as they perform basic functions, such as getting liquidity, offsetting risks and making profits. A given activity can produce profits or losses for another activity. Inefficiencies play the role of food in biological systems, providing profit-making possibilities that support the ecology.[36]

The interaction of heterogeneous actors with different time horizons and a variety of strategies produces the inefficiencies that make up an information gradient. Ecological economics understands the market as a food web, which can be described in terms of a gain matrix defining the interdependencies between different species. At the bottom there are the basal species – slaves, serfs, proletarians, free labour, consumers, account holders, etc. These strata are preyed on by those further up the food chain – pension funds, insurance companies, mutual funds, retail banks; and they in turn feed larger financial institutions, such as hedge funds, brokers, investment banks, propriety trading HFTs, etc. Each financial actor exploits the inefficiencies of the prey species and in the process produces new inefficiencies, further increasing the information gradient. Within this complex ecology there is a gradual stabilisation of predator-prey relationships, but unlike an actual ecosystem, the financial system has a much higher rate of change, leading to more abrupt singular events like flash-crashes evolving according to an accelerated rate of punctuated equilibria, with multiple black swans and mass extinctions.[37]

During the 2010 flash crash, the main US stock index (which is a replica of the market as such) lost about 900 points in a few minutes, recovering most of that loss in the subsequent 15 minutes.[38] To put things into perspective, it represents the wipeout of about $1 trillion in the scope of minutes.[39]

Following the media frenzy around this event, a variety of market actors have rushed to offer explanations for such a one-sided 'social' decision to sell. Part of the explanation lies in a lack of regulatory circuit breakers that would have automatically suspended the free-fall following the abnormally edgy HFT reaction to the discovery of a large 'iceberg' order. From black swans and fat fingers to possible market abuses like quote stuffing (the production of noise in order to obtain a good position in the order book queue), it seems that the causal structure of such events are so complex and opaque that there will never be a definitive explanation. However, we may state with confidence that such occurrences are the kind of irreversible outputs that characterise the hyper-diversity of contemporary socio-technical ecology. Both the SEC-CFTC (2010) report, and the more recent Foresight review have shown that the impetus of the flash crash cannot be traced back to any firm engaged in HFT. Nevertheless, HFT strategies are the present culmination of a tendency towards efficiency of information throughput that inevitably ends up offsetting huge volumes of noise to the wider financial ecology. The question is not so much the good or bad intentions of HFT, but its impact on the resilience and robustness of the overall system. Though speculative trading is often driven by 'fictitious capital' it has real effects in the world, such as food price spikes that may lead to rioting or starvation. As Kliman argues, against underconsumptionist explanations such as David Harvey or Michael Hudson, the current crises are not causally reducible to fictitious finance, rather both are the effects of deeper contradictions within capitalism, indexed by the inexorable tendency of the rate of profit to fall.[40]

Following the sociology of information systems and risk, we could translate this as a result of exchanging high-frequency/low impact events for low-frequency/high impact ones or an exchange between low and high entropy.[41] In this sense, any increase in efficiency (throughput) of one part of the system ends up being dissipated to the rest of the system as noise.[42] If HFT has any part to play in the flash crash, it is because it can be said to represent a real push for efficiency, but one that nevertheless produces unintended consequences for the rest of the financial ecology. In as much as it diminishes the risk of trading through higher matching speeds, HFT allows buyers and sellers to reduce their transaction costs considerably. But the reduction of risk is not actually a reduction as such, and must be understood as a redistribution, or a parametrisation of the fitness landscape of the financial ecology. The crucial point here is that, given the present regulatory framework, which is supported by collusion and corruption at the national and international level (i.e. Federal Reserve, IMF, ratings agencies) a local growth in throughput efficiency enabling the accelerated tapping of low-entropy resources offsets the increased high-entropy to those that are not able to bear it. While the occupants of prime positions on the energy matrix loll around in a rich bath of liquidity, an increasing number are forced to pay for this exuberance with their jobs, their homes, and ultimately their lives. Ray Kurzweil's overzealous enthusiasm for the coming 'singularity', when human 'intelligence' is eclipsed by machines, appears wilfully myopic when we witness the effects of the 'robot phase transition'. Algorithmic hordes of parasitic vampire squids and zombie capitalists compulsively gorge on blood and brains, their exhausted victims lie all around, twitching to the non-periodic outbursts of transient code – the singularity turns out to be just another accelerating extension of exploitation.

Phenomena such as flash crashes are the inevitable outputs of a financial ecology that tends towards the non-linear emergence of noise saturation peaks. At such critical points of friction, something is bound to break. This does not simply apply to market crashes.[43] The present financial ecology maintains an unsustainable rate of throughput and a thanatropic mode of crypsis in the proliferation of strategies for digital subterfuge. In order to address the critical situation of contemporary finance, several liberal beliefs must be overcome: trust in the efficacy of competitive market mechanisms for computing equilibriums, such as the valuation of natural resources and labour; confidence in the capacity of finance to self-regulate, or to be merely a question of discovering the regulatory mechanisms for stabilisation, as it is for Michael Hudson etc.; and faith in the doctrine of sustainable development, which denies the fourth law of thermodynamics. Though finance tends towards efficiency and equity it can never achieve these states since it feeds off the noise created by information asymmetries and structural inequality, and aggressively maintains these disparities in order to extract value from the resulting ecological niches. The demand for transparency is not enough. We should not be placated by a little noise reduction. Friction must be turned around and fed back into the central mechanisms of the system, rather than being dissipated into the margins. As Reza Negarastani argues, we must find 'alternative ways of binding exteriority... remobilized forms of non-dialectical negativity'.[44]

Footnotes

1   Heterodox economics comprises thermo-economics, bio-economics, evolutionary economics and ecological economics; Nicholas Georgescu-Roegen, *The Entropy Law and the Economic Process*, Cambridge, Massachusetts: Harvard University Press, 1971, p.4.
2   Midnight Notes Collective (George Caffentzis, Monty Neill, Hans Widmer, John Willshire), 'The Work/Energy Crisis and the Apocalypse', *Midnight Notes*, Vol. II, #1, 1980.

3   Nicholas Georgescu-Roegen, 'Energy Analysis and Economic Valuation', *Southern Economic Journal*,1979, 45, 4: p.1033.
4   Paul Burkett, *Marxism and Ecological Economics: Toward a Red and Green Political Economy*, Brill, 2006. p.145.
5   The maximum entropy principle is the prime doctrine of Bayesian probability theory, which states that 'the probability distribution which best represents the current state of knowledge is the one with largest information-theoretical entropy.' http://en.wikipedia.org/wiki/Principle_of_maximum_entropy. In the evolutionary economics use of the term, it is thought as one with the 'maximum power principle', as formulated by Jaynes and Lotka, which describes the physics of evolutionary systems. Odum defines it thus: 'During self-organization, system designs develop and prevail that maximize power intake, energy transformation, and those uses that reinforce production and efficiency.' H.T.Odum 'Self-Organization and Maximum Empower', in *Maximum Power: The Ideas and Applications of H.T.Odum*, C.A.S.Hall (ed.), Colorado: Colorado University Press, 1995, p.311.
6   Carsten Herrmann-Pillath, *Foundations of Evolutionary Economics*, Edward Elgar, forthcoming. Available at SSRN: http://ssrn.com/abstract=1781469
7   Stanley Metcalfe and John Foster, Evolution and Economic Complexity, Edward Elgar Publishing, 2007, and Economic Emergence: an Evolutionary Economic Perspective, Max Planck Institute of Economics Jena, Evolutionary Economics Group, # 1112, 2011. This statement should not be taken dogmatically however, since as Ostrum demonstrates there are diverse ways in which collective self-organisation can govern common-pool resource problems that effectively reduce or stop gradients from being tapped at a rate that ends in a 'tragedy of the commons'. Elinor Ostrum, *Governing the Commons: The Evolution of Institutions of Collective Action*, Cambridge University Press, 2008.
8   Michel Callon and Fabian Muniesa,'Les marchés économiques comme dispositifs collectifs de calcul', *Réseaux 21*(122), 2003, pp.189-233.
9   Alan Morrison and William Wilhelm Jr, *Investment Banking: Institutions, Politics, and Law*, Oxford: Oxford University Press, 2nd Revised edition edition, 2008, p.4.
10 Laurence Gialdini and Marc Lenglet, *Financial Intermediaries in an Era of Disintermediation: European Brokerage Firms in a MiFID Context*, 2010, p.23. Available at SSRN: http://ssrn.com/abstract=1616022 or http://dx.doi.org/10.2139/ssrn.1616022
11 Alan Morrison et. al., op. cit., p. 72.
12 J. Doyne Farmer and Spyros Skouras, 'An Ecological Perspective on the Future of Computer Trading', *The Future of Computer Trading in Financial Markets*, UK Foresight Driver Review – DR6, 2011, p.12.
13 Andrei Shleifer and Lawrence Summers, 'The Noise Trader Approach to Finance', *Journal of Economic Perspectives*, Volume 4, Number 2, 1990, pp.19-33.
14 Despite the dialectic of efficiency and inefficiency there is a general trend toward efficiency indexed by the fall in bid-ask spreads. James Angel,Lawrence Harris, and Chster S. Spatt, 'Equity Trading in the 21st Century', Marshall School of Business Working Paper No. FBE 09-10, 2010. Available at SSRN: http://ssrn.com/abstract=1584026 or http://dx.doi.org/10.2139/ssrn.1584026
15 Evan Calder Williams, *Combined and Uneven Apocalypse*, Zero Books, 2011, p.188. Amadeo Bordiga argues that capital functions not just through the 'creative destruction' that Shumpeter identifies, but also through a 'destructive destruction'

necessitated by the build-up of dead labour. Amadeo Bordiga, 'Murder of the Dead', Battaglia Comunista, No. 24 1951; http://marxists.org/archive/bordiga/works/1951/murder.htm
16 Marc Lenglet, 'Conflicting Codes and Codings: How Algorithmic Trading is Reshaping Financial Regulation', Theory, Culture & Society November 2011, 28: 44-66, p.2; Fabian Muniesa, *Des marchés comme algorithmes: sociologie de la cotation électronique à la Bourse de Paris*, Thèse de doctorat (PhD Thesis), Ecole des Mines de Paris, 2003.
17 Ibid., p.3
18 Neil Johnson, Guannan Zhao, Eric Hunsader, Jing Meng, Amith Ravindar, Spencer Carran and Brian Tivnan, 'Financial black swans driven by ultrafast machine ecology', *arXiv*, 7 February 2012.
19 Didier Sornette, *Why Stock Markets Crash*, Princeton University Press, 2003.
20 Michel Callon and Fabian Muniesa,'Les marchés économiques comme dispositifs collectifs de calcul', *Réseaux 21*(122), 2003 or 'Economic Markets as Calculative Collective Devices', *Organization Studies*, 26(8), 2005, p.1236; Alexander R. Galloway, *The Interface Effect*, Polity, 2012. pp. 25-54.
21 Aldridge offers a broad description of different 'algorithmic' classes into electronic, algorithmic, systematic, high-frequency, low-latency, market making, etc. Irene Aldridge, *The Evolution of Algorithmic Classes*, 2010, p. 4.
22 J. Doyne Farmer, Spyros Skouras, *An ecological perspective on the future of computer trading*, p.6
23 Ibid.
24 Ibid., p.16
25 Donald MacKenzie, Daniel Beunza, Yuval Millo, Juan Pablo Pardo-Guerra, *Drilling Through the Allegheny Mountains: Liquidity, Materiality and High-Frequency Trading*, 2012, p.9, http://www.sps.ed.ac.uk/staff/sociology/mackenzie_donald/?a=78186
26 James Angel, Lawrence Harris, Chester S. Spatt, *Equity Trading in the 21st Century*, Marshall School of Business Working Paper No. FBE 09-10, 2010, http://ssrn.com/abstract=1584026 or http://dx.doi.org/10.2139/ssrn.1584026
27 Themis Trading 2008, 2009
28 Donald MacKenzie, op. cit.
29 U. Dieckmanna, P. Marrow, R. Law, 'Evolutionary cycling in predator-prey interactions: population dynamics and the red queen' *Journal of Theoretical Biology*, Volume 176, Issue 1, 7 September 1995, pp.91-102; G. D. Ruxton, T.N. Sherratt & M.P. Speed, 'Avoiding Attack: The Evolutionary Ecology of Crypsis, Warning Signals and Mimicry'. Oxford University Press, 2004.
30 Ray Brassier *Nihil Unbound: Enlightenment and Exctiction*, Palgrave Macmillan 2007, p.43
31 Ibid.
32 Ibid., p.47
33 Foresight: The Future of Computer Trading in Financial Markets (2012) Final Project Report. The Government Office for Science, London
34 Donald MacKenzie, op. cit., p.20
35 Ibid., p.18
36 J. Doyne Farmer, op. cit., p.6.
37 Stephen Jay Gould & Niles Eldredge, 'Punctuated equilibria: the tempo and mode of evolution reconsidered', Paleobiology 3 (2), 115-151, 1977, p.145;. Doyne Farmer, op. cit., p.14.

38 On May 6th 2010, the US stock market experienced one of the most severe price drops in its history; the Dow Jones Industrial Average (DJIA) index dropped almost 9% from the beginning of the day - the second largest point swing, 1,010.14 points, and the biggest one-day point decline, 998.5 points, on an intra-day basis in the history of the DJIA index. Anton Golub, John Keane, *Mini Flash Crashes*, 2011, p1 and Anton Golub, John Keane, Ser-Huang Poon, *High Frequency Trading and Mini Flash Crashes*, HFT Review, 2012, http://arxiv.org/pdf/1211.6667v1.pdf

39 For a time, equity prices of some of the world's biggest companies were in freefall. They appeared to be in a race to zero. Peak to trough, Accenture shares fell by over 99%, from $40 to $0.01. At precisely the same time, shares in Sotheby's rose three thousand-fold, from $34 to $99,999.99. Andrew Haldane, The *race to zero*, International Economic Association Sixteenth World Congress, Beijing, China, 2011, p1, http://www.bankofengland.co.uk/publications/Documents/speeches/2011/speech509.pdf

40 http://thecommune.co.uk/2012/04/29/interview-with-andrew-kliman/

41 Niklas Luhmann, Risk: *A Sociological Theory*, AldineTransaction, 2005; Jannis Kallinikos, *Governing Through Technology: Information Artefacts and Social Practice*. Palgrave Macmillan , Basingstoke, UK, 2011. Claudio Ciborra and O. Hanseth, (eds.) *Risk, complexity and ICT*, Cheltenham: Edward Elgar Publishing, 2007. Elena Esposito, *The Future of Futures: The Time of Money in Financing and Society*, Cheltenham: Edward Elgar Publishing, 2011; Nicholas Georgescu-Roegen, *The Entropy Law and the Economic Process*, Harvard University Press: Cambridge, Massachusetts, 1971

42 Carsten Herrmann-Pillath, *Foundations of Evolutionary Economics*, Edward Elgar, forthcoming. Available at SSRN: http://ssrn.com/abstract=1781469

43 The year 2012 has seen the NASDAQ debacle on the Facebook IPO, the problems with BATS's own IPO and the recent collapse of Knight Capital Group. All of them have been attributed to software problems.

44 Reza Negarastani 'Drafting the Inhuman: Conjectures on Capitalism and Organic Necrocracy' in L.R. Bryant, N. Srnicek, G. Harman (eds.), *The Speculative Turn - Continental Materialism and Realism*, Melbourne: re.press, 2011, p.199.

FIELD NOTES FROM THE CLOUD

SEAN DOCKRAY

Last month, I made a trip to the construction site of the Facebook's first data centre not located in the United States. It is in Luleå, Sweden, a 15 hour train ride north of Stockholm, right by the Arctic Circle. The building is massive – 317 meters long, 100 metres wide, and 15 metres high – you can't see from end to end, as if it has its own vertical horizon. It is based on the same basic layout as their Prineville, Oregon facility – the entire top half of the structure is devoted to cooling. The idea is that cold Arctic air enters and is mixed with hot air produced by running thousands of servers. It is progressively filtered and humidified until it gets to a precise temperature and moisture content, whereupon it is blown through the hot servers to keep them from breaking down.

The first day I visited, a large group of men emerged from a door near the top of the data centre building and descended the temporary staircase in a line. It was probably the closest the building would ever come to its 'workers leaving the factory' moment, because after construction is completed in March, there will be only 30-50 jobs created there. Right now, there are 220 people employed by Swedish construction company, NCC, to build the data centre Originally, the estimate was 300 – but that was based on American techniques, where they build more on site; in Sweden, components are outsourced and shipped to the site, meaning they need fewer hands.

On the other side of the internet from these fat buildings are us and our thin computers, getting thinner by the year. You can picture the evolution: from desktops to laptops to tablets and mobile phones. To make our computers more mobile, processing power and storage is externalised to the cloud. But this distance, this spatial expanse, is overcome by fast connection speeds and smooth interfaces. The devices are literally smooth, so smooth they seem like they were produced by magic, untouched by the human hand; the dominant aesthetic values of user interface design appeals to principles of simplicity, cleanliness, and clarity; and we don't have to wait 30 seconds for the modem song to be connected. More and more, it's a question of how many wireless networks there are, or how many bars we have, not whether or not we're connected.

The Facebook construction site is carved out of the forest, as if the trees have been shaved off like a beard. There are supposed to be three giant buildings here eventually, each containing four server halls, where the actual computers will do their thing. But for now, there is just the first building and a hole carved out of the forest where the rest might be someday.

These servers are meant to handle traffic from Europe and the Middle East. This means that the so-called 'Facebook revolutions' (like those protests and popular revolutionary movements in Iran, Egypt and Tunisia) would happen here, in Luleå. At least in part. There are many reasons for building the data centre here and one of the most important ones is that Sweden is politically stable. The risk analysis people say that the odds are Sweden won't have any kind of revolution itself; and therefore it's a safe investment. The air is cold, so to speak.

I became interested in data centres last year after coming across an interior photograph – the server racks have a striking resemblance to library stacks. When you think about the thin computers – Kindles and iPads, for example – as books, the comparison becomes even more unsettling. (The proliferation of data centres comes at just the moment that library collections are being deaccessioned, staff and opening hours cut, and some branches closed entirely.) On these devices, a person needs to agree to certain 'terms of service', possess a unique, measurable account, and provide payment information; in return, access is granted. This access is not ownership in the conventional sense of a book, or even the digital sense of a file, but rather a license that gives the person a 'non-exclusive right to keep a permanent copy [...] solely for your personal and non-commercial use', contradicting the First Sale Doctrine, which gives the 'the right to sell', lease, or rent their copy to anyone they choose at any price they choose. Such contradictions are symptoms of the shift in property regimes, or what Jeremy Rifkin called 'the age of access'. He writes that 'property continues to exist but is far less likely to be exchanged in markets. Instead, suppliers hold on to property in the new economy and lease, rent, or charge an admission fee, subscription, or membership dues for its short-term use.'[1]

Of all the reasons Facebook ended up in northern Sweden, the single most important one is the Lule River and the cheap hydroelectric power that it generates in 15 power plants along its length. It used to take decades for the cost of electricity to exceed the cost of a server and so electricity was a marginal expense. But now, it is only a few years until the cost of running the thing costs more than the thing itself, making electricity decisive.

It also used to be that buildings requiring a lot of power, a paper mill or a factory for example, would have to be situated near to a river in order to generate enough to push the machinery into motion. With motors and electrical power stations and high voltage transmission lines, a factory could be situated almost anywhere as long as it was hooked up to a source of electricity. The sources of power could be more and more distant, in places one would rarely visit.

Microsoft (who has moved quite deliberately into data centres) released a publication three years ago about the 'fourth paradigm' in science, which observes that most important scientific research is now engaged with observing, analysing and visualising data, rather than the material world. We discover new diseases and their cures looking through computers. And this data, a model of the world and its phenomena, is stored and processed in data centres Here is the cloud – not confined to scientific data, but everything abstracted into data – business transactions, music and film, correspondences, personal photos, and so on.

About 30 kilometres north of Luleå is the closest plant, in Boden. The Facebook data centre will consume as much electricity as the small city of Boden does. And data centres worldwide consumed as much energy as the entire country of Sweden – or they did three years ago. It seems as though the scale of data centres is so large and their activity so opaque that we constantly make these comparisons to make sense of it. Heidegger wrote about hydroelectric plants on the Rhine in his 'Question Concerning Technology' – in contrast to the windmill, which directly converts wind into energy, the hydroelectric plant stores up the energy of the river to be converted at will – nature has become a resource, a thing for human use rather than simply a thing in itself.

It's difficult to tell at all if anyone is working at these power stations. In one video that I saw on the internet, it featured a woman who would drive around Norrboten County and check up on the infrastructure to make sure that everything was OK. Once they're built there's really not much of a need for anyone to actually be there – in fact, it is probably a liability for someone to be there because what if they get bored, or angry about the terms of their last contract? This is probably how it will be with Facebook, once the data centre is completed – there will be very few workers who are employed not to keep things running, that's something else, but to stop things from falling apart.

The biggest investment in Luleå, prior to the data centre, was the steel mill built in 1940, now operated by SSAB. A railway connects the mill to iron ore mines in the mountains to the north west – LKAB trains roll in several times a day delivering product from Malmberget and Kiruna. There, much of the drilling and shuttling is done with automation and remote control. Since the late 1970s, the Swedish steel industry has been restructured, which means that more computer control has been introduced, and many jobs eliminated. At that time, the entire industry was 'in trouble,' or, in other words, they weren't profitable.

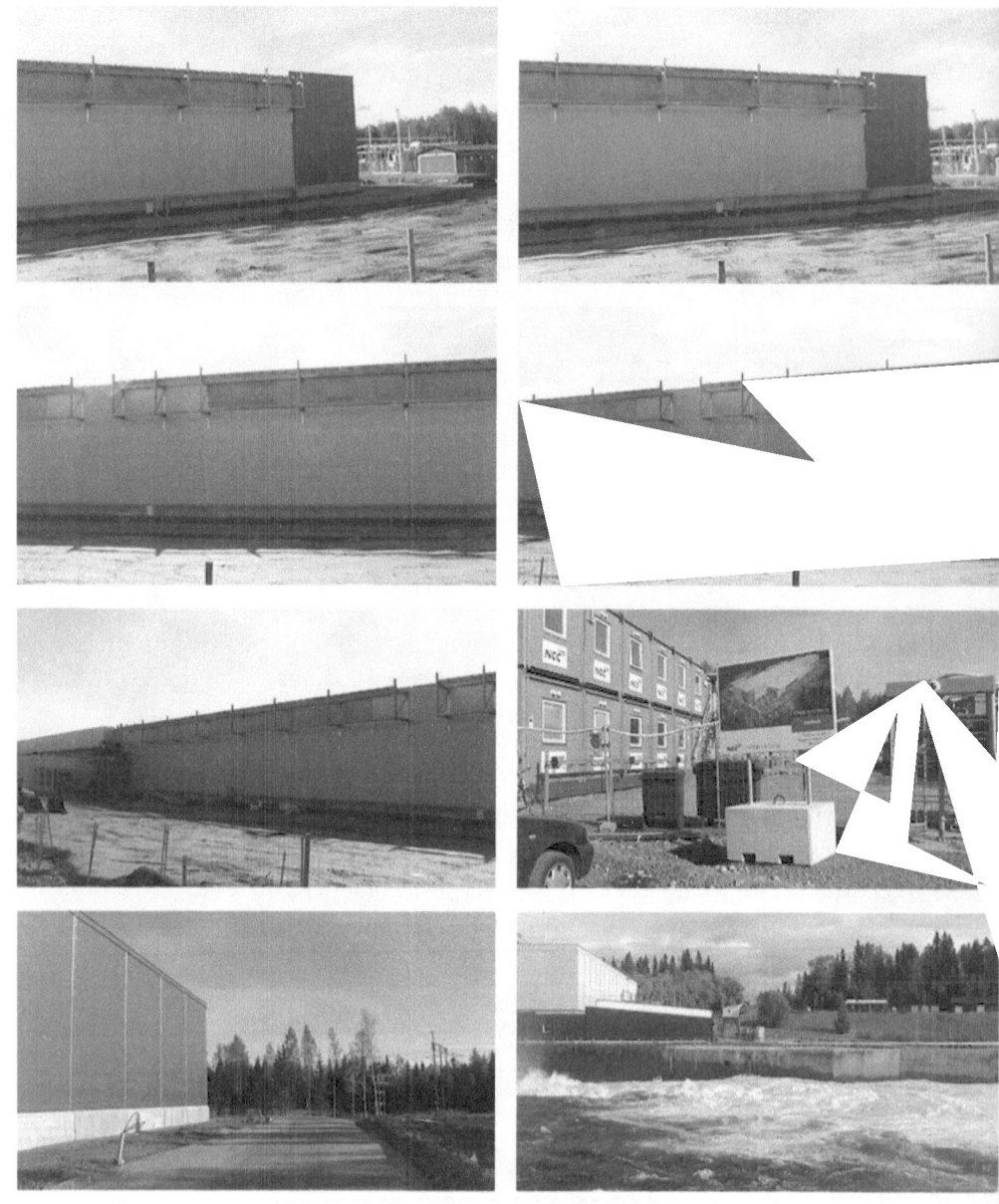

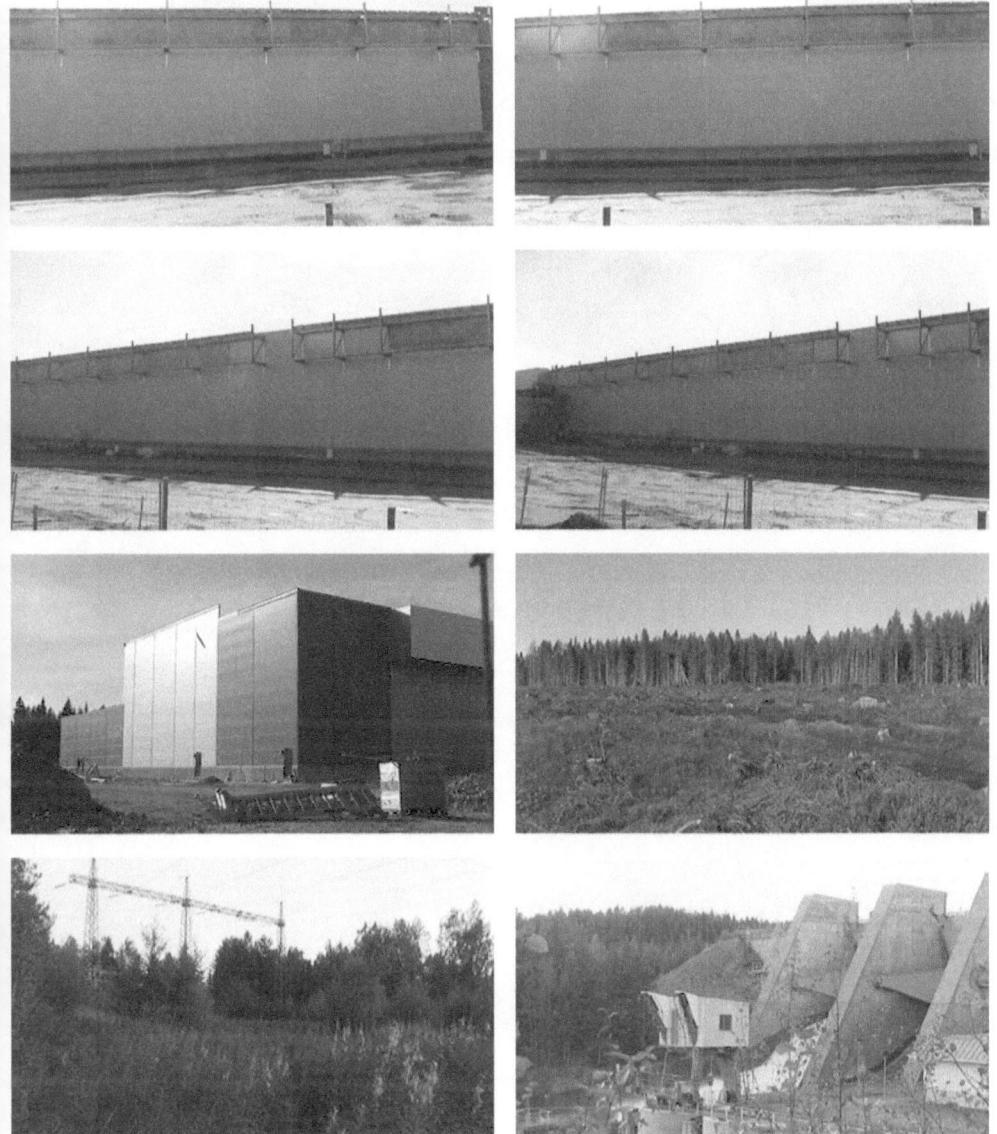

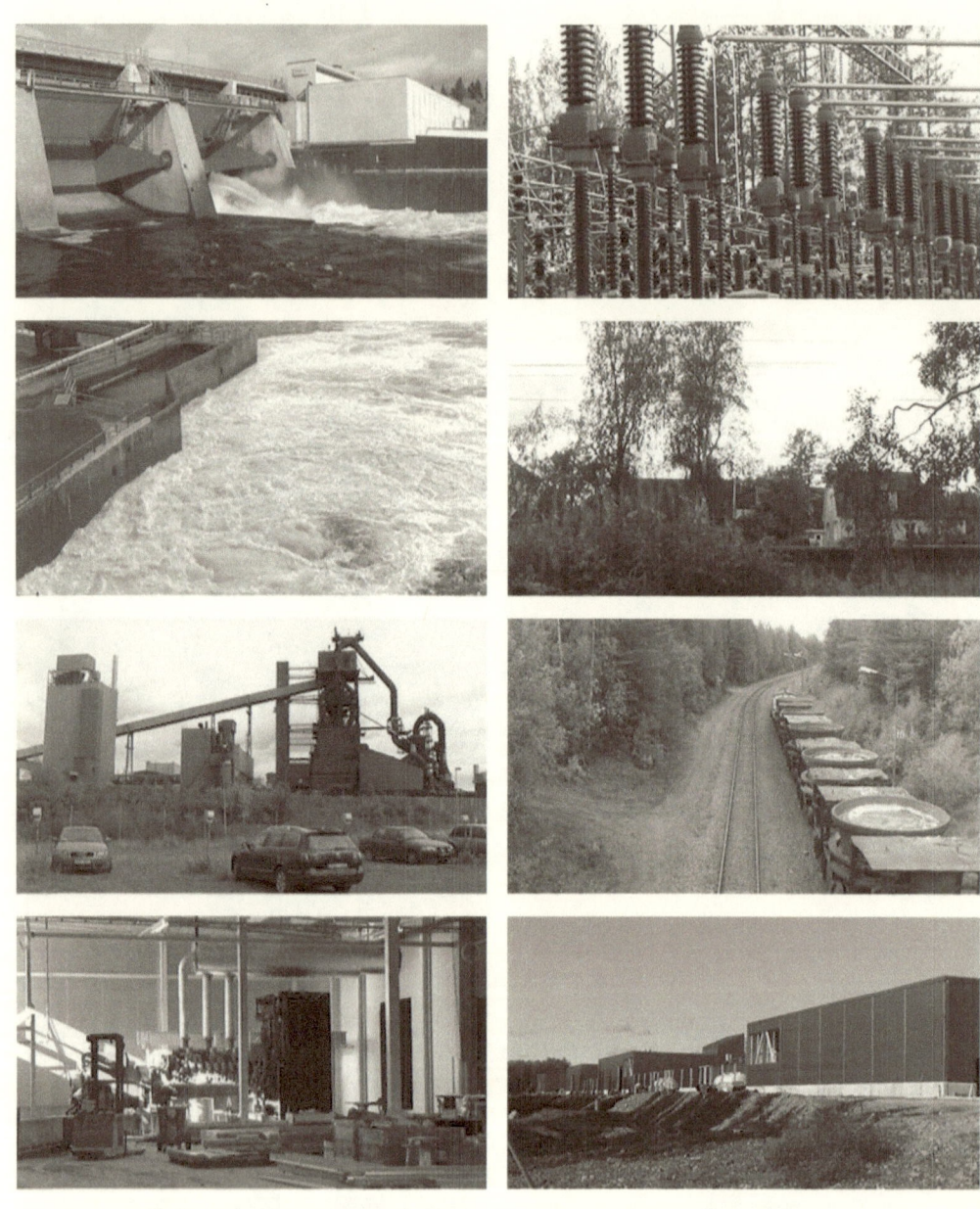

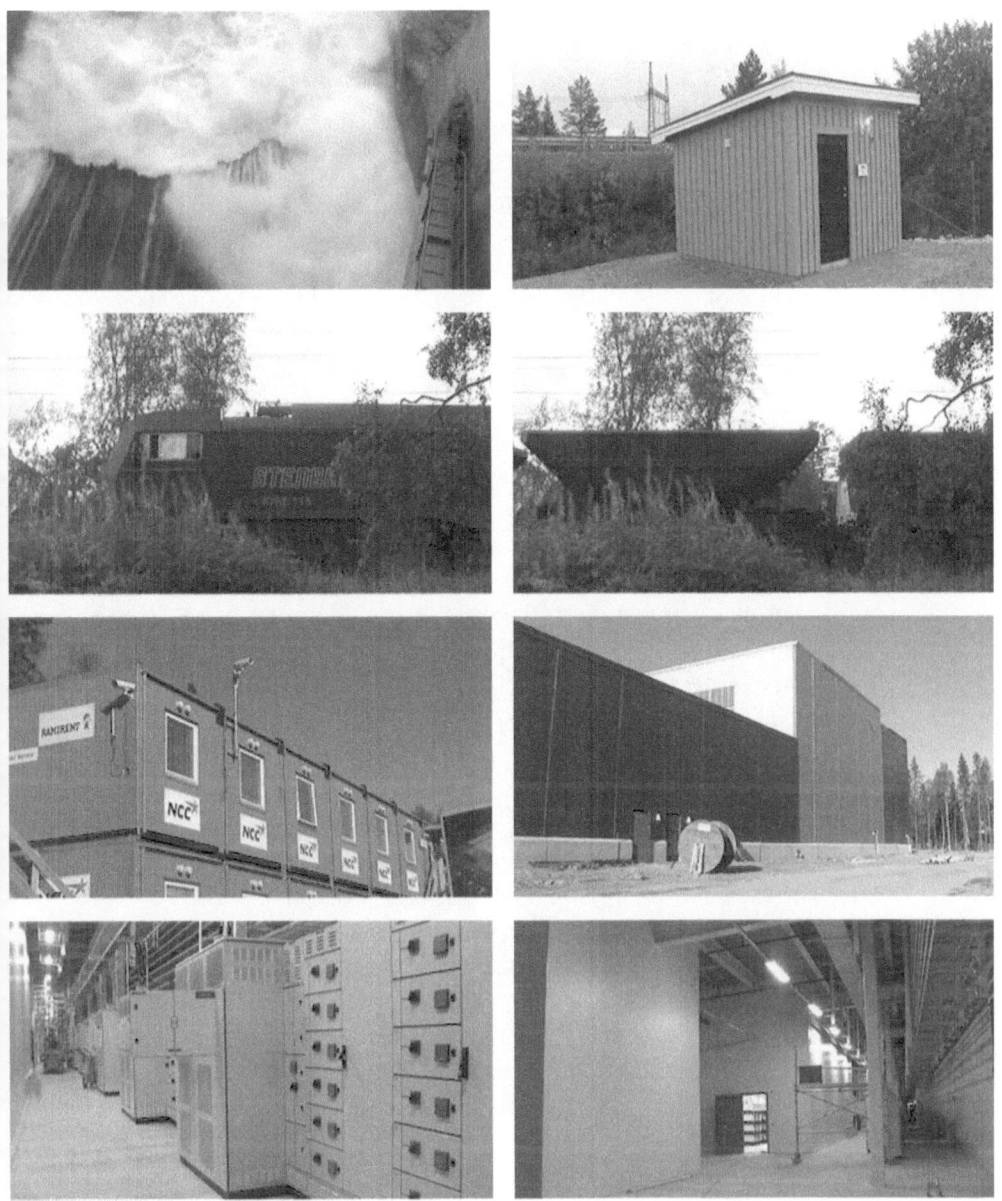

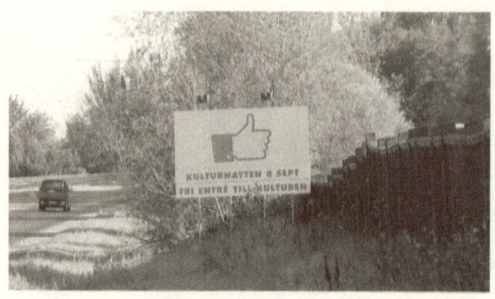

There's a video of one of the engineers building the Prineville Facebook data centre who says, 'this is a factory, it's just a different kind of factory than you might be used to.' I think that the SSAB steel mill is the kind of factory he is talking about. The steel mill seems almost proud compared to the data centre. It is visible, upright, and muscular. Something from a past era really; or maybe a passing era. The data centre is monstrous; an absurdity in the landscape, trying to be discreet, trying to move in without drama and then keep to itself. It doesn't give much of itself – in fact all it really does is collect data. Its workers are spread across the globe, usually bent in front of a computer, but more often now staring into the palm of their hand. They enter data, upload 100 million photographs per day, and the data centre has to be always on to collect it all.

The future of Luleå is not in steel, it is in data. They've rebranded the area the Node Pole to attract other technology companies to bring their data here. They are advertising one site right next to the SSAB steelworks. Another site is in a former sawmill. A paradigm shift, say the business people.

When I visited, the people in the blue offices refused to give me a tour or let me visit the building. I found out later that a Google executive had surreptitiously gone on a tour and taken some photographs prior to my arrival, resulting in a minor scandal. Data centres are supposed to be very secure.

They store an immense amount of equipment and technology and within that they store an immense amount of data. Really, they are constructing a mine. There will be valuable raw material in there somewhere, but no one knows quite what it is yet. 100 million photographs are uploaded to the mine every day, and they want to know what's really in there. Algorithms trying to figure out what structures exist underneath and through the ones that we can see? Or, maybe it's not a mine, but a power plant for human resources. Our social energy as a resource that can be stored and used at will.

This data centre would be the placid side of the dam and the algorithms are the things that open the gates and convert all of that social movement into energy, into work and into profit.

No one knows how many data centres there are on the planet, but estimates say from half a million to three million. Because they require so much capital investment, decisions on where to locate them are not based on sentimentality, ethics, or ideology, but on risk and cost-benefit analysis. They spread across the planet according to an autonomous logic outside of direct human control. They find unlikely places, occupy relics of the 20th century like Model T factories, limestone mines, printing presses, military bunkers, even shopping malls. One can't help but wonder how many there will be when this is all over - will the age of data centres ever be over? - What kind of super-ruins will splatter the landscape? Will the data have been migrated to a less hostile climate? Or will bits of it remain, left for the future archeologists of the fourth paradigm?

What kind of culture can we produce on these platforms? We typically say they are merely tools for organising and publicity, no different than say, a cell phone or a poster, and that we would simply make use of whatever was available. But I think that the restructuring that's occurring is much deeper than that - in the same way that a lab culture that used to be in a petri dish is now in a data centre, it seems as though so much culture (artist-run or otherwise) is platformed.

Where does one draw the lines between: (1) platforms that one is willing to use. (2) alternative platforms that should be constructed in place of hegemonic or corporate ones. (3) activities that must resolutely reside outside of computation and digital networks? Even within and across these divisions there are further subdivisions, recombinations, and movements.

Footnotes

1 Jeremy Rifkin, *The Age of Access: The New Culture of Hypercapitalism, Where All of Life Is a Paid-for Experience*, 2000, http://www.dmmserver.com/DialABook/978/158/542/9781585420186.html

SEAMLENS

GORDAN SAVIČIĆ

Seamlens is a tool meant to render visible the hidden network processes that take place between smartphone devices and cloud services. It captures and performs network analysis on a standard Android handheld device. The title Seamlens reflects on the *seamlessness* of network traffic through the lens of a deep network inspection. The concept of *seamlessness* is crucial to the contemporary so-called rich user-experience of mobile applications. It is a design approach whose implementation traverses all user interactions. Most applications are seamlessly integrated into the user experience which makes them comfortable to use. While social media technologies were developing rapidly, there was very little understanding of what it physically means to be part of the cloud on a mobile device. We suddenly realise that cyberspace is no longer the 'elsewhere' far away behind our computer screens, but that it has neatly moved into our pocket as smart devices connecting our social space and physicality around us with the so-called 'cloud'. Hence, it is difficult even for experienced users to grasp the background processes within the protocological network. It became hard to differentiate which data is a 'local' reference point and which part of the interaction is stored and processed through cloud services and remote server locations.

While not offering a solution, Seamlens attempts to cast light on our scattered multi-device personalities. The app of the same name was developed to constantly capture in- and outgoing network traffic from an Android phone when the user is not actively engaging with the device (mostly browsing). Smart-devices constantly update and interact with a multitude of servers. Irrespective of physical constraints, this traffic spans over vast distances, from the user's current location to remote server farms, moving back and forth. The physical location of these services is a starting point for this investigation.

The app geo-locates all IP addresses the device communicates with. This information is captured and translated into a map visualisation which can be explored interactively on the device. It uses a modified layer of Open Street map, based on Leaflet. The map geolocates the destination and source for traffic exchange. It gives an overview of traffic size, protocols in use and the real owners of the associated servers. The map still lacks any sort of indicator for the new forms of economisation and valorisation of network traffic and metadata tracking. It does, however, highlight our network dependency on private companies and the enormous amount of machine to machine communication.

The project title is a word play on a particular kind of prism named the 'Lüneburg lens': a spherical multi-layered lens which is capable of focusing a wave from any direction. In a similar way, Seamlens focuses user interactions from any direction within the network topology. It takes the user as a focal point and performs real-time interpolation of two given concentric spheres, the earth and its interwoven cloud of permanent connectivity. Seamlens is still in beta and some functions are waiting to be implemented.

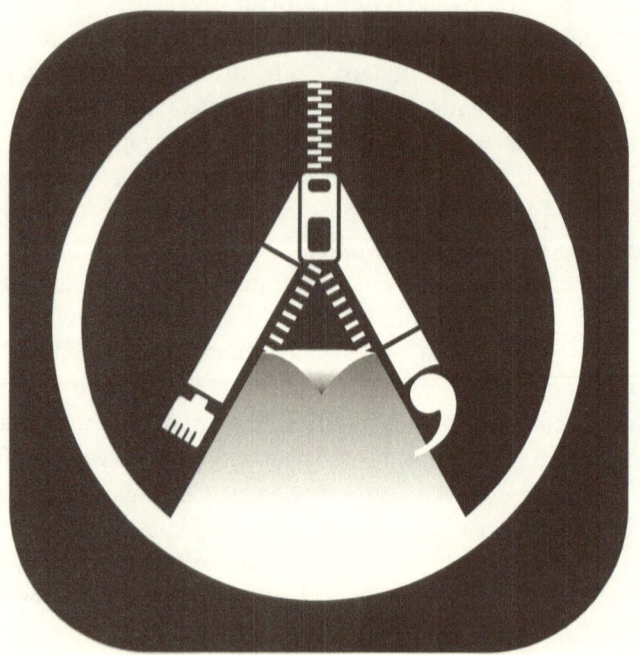

Gordan Savičić Seamlens mobile app icon, 2013
All images and diagrams are under GNU Free Documentation License v1

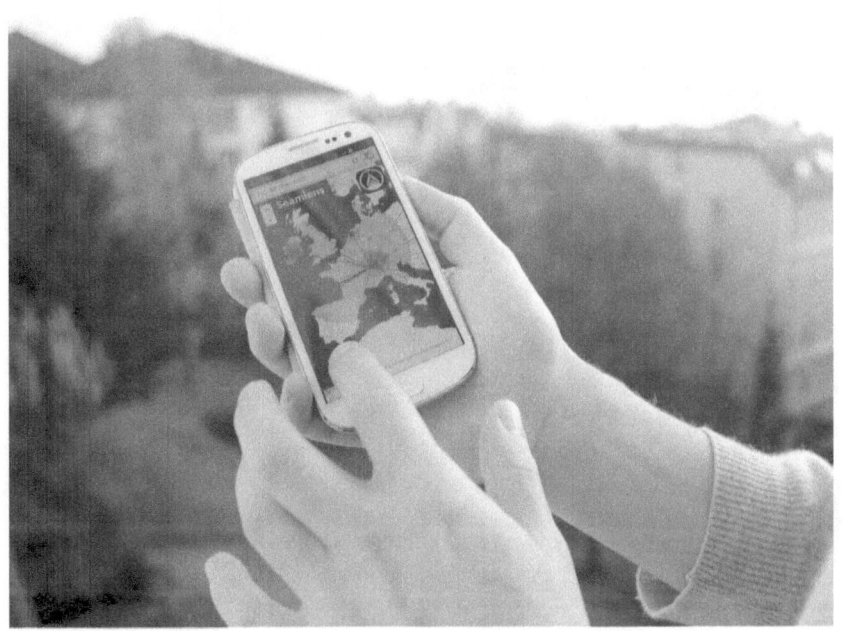

Gordan Savičić, Mobile map view of Seamlens user, 2013

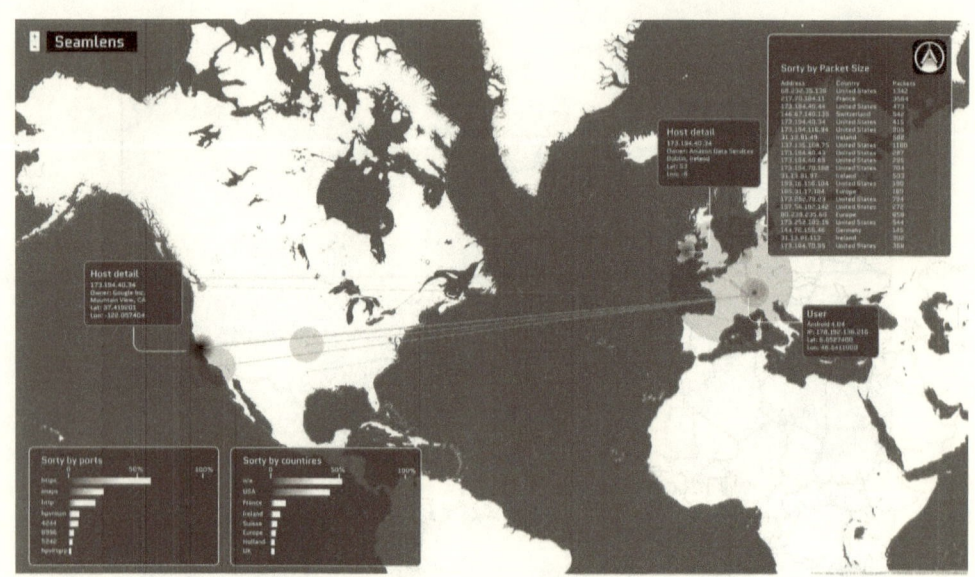
Gordan Savičić, Mobile map view of Seamlens user, 2013

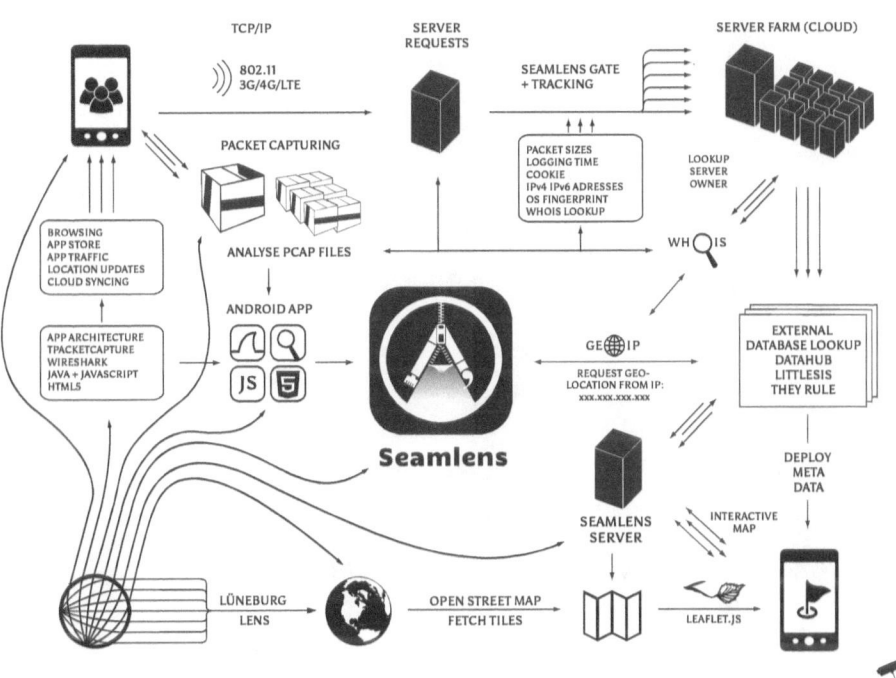

Gordan Savičić, Seamlens network diagram / Exploit overview, 2013

THE QUESTION OF ORGANISATION AFTER NETWORKS

The idea of the 'self-organising network' has reshaped politics and notions of agency in models of the environment, cognitive science, warfare, government, grassroots activism and even service provision. How does this embrace of the network paradigm beyond its technological fundament coincide with economic, social and epistemological shifts? How have the promulgation and critique of networked organising, circulated on the web and in activist circles, impacted our ideas of good or efficacious social organisation? What forms of emergent organisation are moving beyond the aporias of the network?

The proliferation of social institutions (education, medicalisation, culture, care, etc.) has long been critiqued as producing social and psychic dependencies, normativities and appropriations of the subject in accordance with the logics of state/capitalism – expanding exponentially to organise and format human life. However, we are now undergoing their mass disassembly under the neoliberal model of restructuring. Can we rethink autonomous activity, subjects or agencies in this climate, resisting a collusion with the contracted state brought on by neoliberal ideology and austerity? Can we update historical adventures in alternative, autonomous or autodidact institutions and practices within the context of the net and its many knowledge sharing potentials?

IMMANENCE AFTER NETWORKS

RÓZSA ZITA FARKAS

December 2013

Organisation of Immanence

In my research proposal for the Post-Media Lab's 'Organisation After Networks' theme, I reflected on Jodi Dean's description of 'communicative capitalism' and the argument that online interactions can only oil the cogs of capital and reduce the potential for radical action. Building on this original proposal I decided that, for my research question, 'organisation' would mean organisation of and by radical subjectivities, and if and how they produce rupture within the biopolitical status quo – most specifically through aesthetics. I have focused on art practices that are largely and most effectively played out online – often across platforms such as Tumblr – despite them being explicitly and directly related to corporations.[1] A pertinent question, when looking at the manifestation of radical subjectivities, became if and how so-called 'feminine aesthetics' in art practices can act as a vessel for radicalisation, and be a viable way of deploying feminism within biopowerful, patriarchal, systems.[2] Part of my research for Post-Media Lab (PML) became the question of whether feminine aesthetics are in fact, feminist. This question acts as a prerequisite for the text, due to the direct gendering of the terminology.

From the perspective of a curator, I began to define a type of radical action (or 'organisation') as a shift in aesthetic culture (a resurgence of feminine aesthetics), and sought to understand whether this in itself fundamentally challenges patriarchal space. As put by Dean, 'the multitude' builds on Spinozian *potentia* (power), which offers up immanence as a process with revolutionary potential. Is a radical shift in culture simply an adoption of immanence, as in, potentially radical, yet ultimately ineffective? This ineffectiveness could be one logical consequence of a view: that there is no outside of empire (Hardt & Negri, Dean). Dean asserts 'Hardt and Negri see the whole of empire as an "open site of conflict" [and as] an asset insofar as it releases opposition from the pressure of organization and prevents co-optation.'[3] This view, within a landscape of 'capitalist realism', builds upon the postmodern view that the future no longer holds a promise of difference, or of progress outside the foundations of capitalist exchange and is, instead, effectively imploded as a concept, which 'makes itself felt affectively as political impotence.'[4]

Although noteworthy work has been done on immanence, aside from theories of the multitude, and from a more focused subject position in Affect Theory (by Brian Massumi, Melissa Gregg, Sara Ahmed and others), the retort still remains that immanence itself is largely unmoved or ineffective within structures, and has instead become largely subsumed by its own circulation and commodification, as seen in the post-'68 rise of revolution as the personal, or individual pursuit, of 'owning' one's identity. Or to put it more candidly, the fetishisation of counterculture via surface signifiers. If immanence is the productive ground by which potential is produced, then that ground is being rented out wholesale. Immanence itself, in its supposed opposition to transcendence, is predicated upon its immersion within material reality – immanence is a state within the very fibres of reality and core of our relations. Its relationship to the material realities of capitalism, in forms such as affective labour, is clear. Immanence mutates and embeds itself according to the system it is located within, and has become holistically embedded into processes of commodification under capital.

Affect is by definition present in external relationships, or effects between or upon agents. If this is part of the essence, or commodified object of immanence, then, following Hardt and Negri, I understand these relationships as part of a mesh, subsumed and under the skin of biopower, as opposed to operating simply between two agents. I wish to imagine embeddedness as a metaphor for infiltration rather than subsumption, envisaging these processes in networks as spatial. Immanence now rejects its difference from transcendence, offers ossified moments of affect, and performs as if apparently on its own 'plane', on top of a context that is totally mediated. Under the guise of ineffective *potentia*, immanence pretends it is unbridled and detached, that it is *pure*, whilst, and following on from discussions surrounding communicative capitalism, it stays within, as it always was.[5] If immanence, in pretence of purity, is more embedded than ever, and our online interactions are underpinned by the exchange of capital within networks, then does affect within aesthetics have a chance of penetrating space, or acting as a Temporary Autonomous Zone, in web 2.0?[6]

Self-Reification

In Facebook, Tumblr, Twitter, et al., our self, even as avatar, is chiefly predicated upon a gendered individual identity. Performativity is the sociological order of the day, and affect often acts as the reifying, concurrent feature of artwork performed across these platforms. Georg Lukács defined reification as the process whereby a social relation becomes a thing – and it is here that a feminine aesthetic can risk 'real subsumption' and the evacuation of its feminist potential.[7] This danger is also seen when, as is

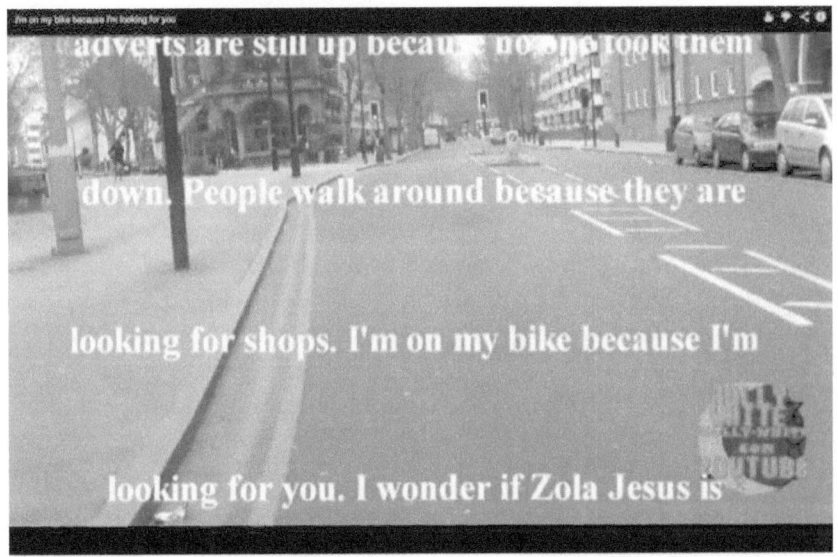

Screenshot from Holly White's *I'm on my bike because I'm looking for you*, 2013

frequently the case in contemporary aesthetics, the network, the internet is reified as a thing, or object in itself. This lifts one structure from a discourse on power under empire, as biopowerful and inseparable form 'intra-acting agencies'.[8] Examples of this in specific artworks often occur when the reification happens through replication, such as with Brad Tromel's *Silk Road Objects* (2011-ongoing), or in the recent exhibition by artist Johann Arens, *Internet Centre and Habesha Grocery*:

> At Internet Centre & Habesha Grocery, every desk partition became a temporary office for those without one to go to.
>
> An installation with the same name at Paradise Row will combine remains of the café's interior with an array of standard exhibition furniture.[9]

Feminine aesthetics do not so much self-reify via replication of an outside 'thing'; the aesthetics are produced in the replication of lived subjectivities, such as in Ann Hirsch's autobiographical play, *Playground*, or Mary Bond's *autodissociate.me* net.art piece. Works such as Hirsch and Bond's are opposed to replicating a thing that is adopted, or approached, as something external to one's own (embodied) subjectivity. Yet the still inherent risks of reification are precisely why I find emerging feminine aesthetics so engaging. Penetrative reification, seen in the use of affect as a medium in art practices, is often invested in the Latourian idea of tracing the movement of the network, via the diaristic and social qualities of many moments in networked cultural capital, objectifying the social into a reified essence, whilst at the same time de-reifying, reflecting back onto, critiquing and utilising this process. This happens through the sheer extent of cross-platform production – of multi-mediums (of the post-media condition), by frisking various expanded fields until we, the reader, are at a loss as to which moment, image, woman, object is the 'true' reified commodity.

The obscuring of reification (although not removing it) treats affect *as within* and highlights the rendition of pure immanence under capital, entering a dialogue with biopower and attempting to control one's own objectification. It can be an act of agency of the self, in part an act of female transgression; a performance fractured and splayed across locations. The historical and present gendering of affect (as female) allows for an insertion of femaleness into neutral (patriarchal) space in this guise, particularly in artworks that perform across multiple platforms which are easily accessible, at least in comparison to 'legitimate' art spaces. Insertion into neutral space is carried out within this process of reification, or the pastiche of pure immanence, but the risk is that whilst penetrating neutrality, a *feminine aesthetic* is nevertheless contained *only* as a commodity, or value-form.

The value-form is being totalised – distinctly in our social relations, and thus identities – yet it has also encountered a fissure. The value-form has been multiplied and spread thinly everywhere and into everything. Yet Fukyama's end of history is even doubted by the banks, the future as realistically capitalist is not so convincing, the loans aren't doled out. Capitalism, as a system, is being questioned on both sides – of course in different ways.[10] What has happened to the value-form, and what we see in the emerging art practices I am invested in is, following Katja Diefenbach, a much more engaged and spectral form of value.[11] This broken, spectral form, or art made from the material of affect, is deployed in a 2013 YouTube video work by Holly White; titled, *I'm on my bike because I'm looking for you*. Here her incorporation of the site of distribution into the artwork and/or the radical subjectivity she inhabits draws out the spectre of value, which was always there. 'Use' and 'exchange' values are not so dichotomous, they are in fact as abstract and oblique as each other – superimposed by way of narrative: the bike-as-protagonist, the 'shops' as loss of site; or Zola Jesus playing on her mp3, and 'Half Price Cava' as empty sign. When describing the literary critic and Harvard professor, Barbara Johnson, Lauren Berlant points out that a fake moment of *intersubjectivity* can create the conditions for an address to take place.[12] A designated rendition of affect is what much of the performative, feminine aesthetics provide.

Holly White's video depicts the moving view of cycling through South London. The film uses a point-of-view shot of the artist herself who is filming while cycling. The message: 'I'm on my bike because I'm looking for you', spills over the footage, the loss of future or past is real in this work, perhaps utopian, perhaps dystopian; emotions transform into a rejection of the structural governance of exchange-value. 'It still says Half Price Cava on the wall of the Co-op but it's not Half Price any more. They ran out of Cava. They ran out of all the food and now it's shut. All the shops are shut. But the adverts are still up because no one took them down.'[13]

The expansion of the artwork's objecthood, self-production and distribution, can be viewed within the terms of immaterial labour as defined by Maurizio Lazzarato, and specifically in regard to the (digital) materials, and (online) exposition spaces at hand for many of these works – in particular due to the works' precise entanglement with the communicative capitalism that produces these spaces and materials. In Lazzarato's definition:

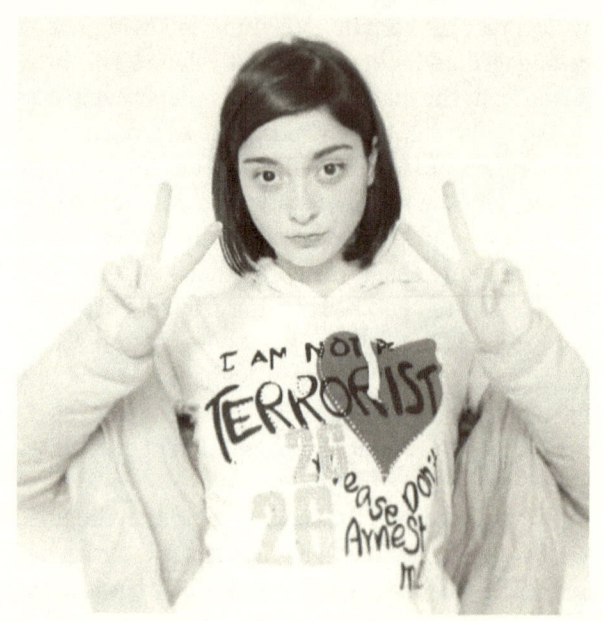

Amalia Ulman's euro-store inspired fashion selfie, from her facebook

[T]he labor that produces the informational and cultural content of the commodity. The concept of immaterial labor refers to two different aspects of labor. On the one hand, [. . .] skills involving cybernetics and computer control (and horizontal and vertical communication). On the other hand, as regards the activity that produces the 'cultural content' of the commodity, immaterial labor involves a series of activities that are not normally recognized as 'work' – in other words, the kinds of activities involved in defining and fixing cultural and artistic standards, fashions, tastes, consumer norms, and, more strategically, public opinion.[14]

Yet importantly, the distinct promise of emotion, and the additional reproduction of these works – as they travel via shares and re-blogs – doesn't solely build the capital of the commodity, or traditional value-form alone. The image itself performs affective labour, cultivating sociality and providing work that is intrinsic to the social fabric, creating emotional experiences in people. The strongest means used to play and move art objects across material and information networks is the reification of affect itself. What is meant in terms of the network, or context of the image, is its indexing to conventional meanings in an intersubjective context, its socio-linguistic and technical qualification. This qualification of language and/or images doesn't operate singularly, as representation, but rather as one moment in biopower itself, or a relation within a schema such as Karen Barad's agential realism: a performative, experiential representation, which can only be made within the context of history too.[15] Thus the performative transgression and occupation of neutral space cannot refuse or ignore the performer's own gender if we are to move beyond the biopolitics interpellated into us.

Many works such as White's are not yet wholly formed commodities or actions. The core of affection is situated in the space in between content and effect, as Massumi has argued.[16] The spectral form of the art object relies upon the surfaces of what Lauren Berlant calls 'cruel optimism', 'with its suppression of the risks of attachment. A change of heart, a sensorial shift, intersubjectivity', or, the iterations of a practice that skirts across and is encapsulated by the state of crisis of everyday life, where optimism is cruel, giving false utopias within the crisis.[17] Feminine aesthetics in particular exist in this context, engaging in a tantalisingly cruel optimism, whilst also attempting to offer a realism of representation: the crisis as everyday, bound in 'a kind of relation in which one depends on objects that block the very thriving that motivates our attachment in the first place.'[18] As laid out by Berlant, this total reification is on one hand the provision of a lens onto the crisis of the everyday; and instigator of some form of resistance on the other. Yet also, as with feminine aesthetics, it is still embedded and so, unable to fix the problem – it merely magnifies it.

Optimism Reproduced

To further interrogate whether the double-edged, cruelly optimistic (art) object holds feminist potential, we must remind ourselves of the element of reproduction within affective labour. The forms of interaction termed 'communicative capitalism', such as the process by which Holly White's video is posted onto others' Facebook walls, can also be read as the pure reproduction of affect and the (free) conditions or provision of emotional fabric for a labour force. Affective labour as a theory owes much of its construction to the work of Italian autonomist feminist theorists, and bound as it is with work on immaterial labour under empire, it is also distinct and gendered. Many are noticing the trend and proliferation of feminine aesthetics, yet their development is critically questioned. As put in a recent *Art F City* article:

> Several respondents spoke up to express concern about a type of overly feminine net art that's grown increasingly popular over the last four or five years. This can include the glossy skinned, 3-D rendered self-portraits; the sentimental teenage girl selfies and webcam vids; the cutesy anime girl posturing; and the colour pink, all of which seem devoid of a critical position – or a stance of any kind – just replicating what we already see and know around the web.[19]

Such 'concern' is understandable. The artist Darja Bajagić's work, which appropriates found images of women from the internet, says it is 'far from seeking to deal directly with these historically embedded issues, [instead it] employs the images as ciphers to explore other, more abstract ideas.'[20] The repetitious use of the female body by Bajagić, is, as with Tromel's *Silk Road Objects*, a repetition of a 'thing'. It is presented as able to transcend the subjectivity or power relations within which it exists, or it 'supersedes the patriarchal fallacy of feminine mystery. The collective imagery inhabits an intense blankness [...] the neutralising force of generalisation.'[21]

Whilst passing moral judgement on the attempted escape from the ghettoisation the art world imposes on feminist art is not helpful, and is certainly levelled at male artists far less, it is indeed questionable whether we can totally avoid the biopolitical context in which Bajagić's images are garnered. In contrast to readings of Bajagić's work, I think that it is precisely the 'feminisation', or use of affect, rather than neutralisation or generalisation, which can inject position into the field.

Opening up neutral space (deterritorialising the masculine), as opposed to hiding within it, is broached by the affective gaps, dissemination of subjectivity into landscape, and immanence un-pure, rather than repetition-for-generalisation. Seeing affect as not simply being, but moving, acting as a means to open up the *Thirdspace*, as opposed to adapting to the neutral.[22] The key difference in the concern proposed around a feminine aesthetic, and the practice of artwork that seeks to generalise the female body, is that although both display a methodology for resistance, shown by critic Elvia Wilk's essay on the gendering of the posthuman, the spatial and structural conditions around which gender is formed mean that it is not enough to simply reject our bodies.[23] A feminine aesthetic, whose commonality is the trail, or ebullition of affect, holds more potential for collective radical subjectivity, than the rejection of the feminine. But what is feminine, why speak in these terms? Nelly Richard's book *Masculine/Feminine*, rather than disputing the binary – zero or one – which masculine and feminine occupy (a binary whose history was importantly renegotiated by Sadie Plant) asks us to think outside of binaries and into plurality. For Richard, women join together, which provides a 'we' that 'feminism must also learn to deconstruct'.[24] For Richard, the deconstruction of the female 'we' is necessary 'to inflect its mark as a plural staging of interventions and confrontations between identities, genders, sexes, cultures, languages and forms of power. This gesture needs to be made plural so as to communicate rather than isolate.'[25]

Richard's 'intersectionality' via deconstruction is of its moment – postmodernism – yet the deconstructed, plural feminines are now ubiquitous (online), and having moved through this we can learn to maintain the transgression argued for by Richard, whilst re-collectivising into a 'we', and activating plural feminines further, by the penetration of neutrality. This is not to say one must refuse Practices of Difference in order to become 'we' – a one-size-fits-all feminine is, as Richard shows, undesirable, yet although individual transgression seems to be an attainable preoccupation of postmodern deconstruction, our plural selves are left wandering upon a one-size-fits-all structure. We are yet to be provided with the *space* for The Other to live – that space must be taken, through structural transgression and enforced by collective-pluralities.

we are the modern cunt
positive anti reason
unbounded unleashed unforgiving
we see art with our cunt we make art with our cunt
we believe in jouissance madness holiness and poetry
we are the virus of the new world disorder
rupturing the symbolic from within
saboteurs of big daddy mainframe
the clitoris is a direct line to the matrix
the VNS MATRIX
terminators of the moral code
mercenaries of slime
go down on the altar of abjection
probing the visceral temple we speak in tongues
infiltrating disrupting disseminating
corrupting the discourse
we are the future cunt

VNS Matrix's, *A Cyberfeminist Manifesto for the 21st Century*, 1991

Feminist Art 1.0

In order to explore the embodiment displayed in new feminine aesthetics, I wish to look at the history of this tool within feminist art. As an example, Judy Chicago's *The Dinner Party* (1979), contains many signifiers that can be recognised in the practice of young women artists today. Autonomist feminists repeatedly asserted that the primary space of affective labour is the domestic or private sphere, the home. Chicago's exaggerated presentation of this moment of domesticity and caregiving (the dinner party) in a public institution, along with her gathering of public and historical figures into a collective domestic 'scenario', shares the perspective of Leopoldina Fortunati's critique of reproduction as state-controlled, unpaid, and affective labour. The 'private' space of the home is in fact public and systemic to capitalist labour systems. The ramifications of domestic-as-public space is imbued in the technologies used by artists today – namely self-branding via social media, the idea that one's private life is a commodity that ties narrative into art practices. Although much of this work may not explicitly critique the domestic-as-public sphere it nevertheless brings it into view. Such recent practices also give a nod to Chicago's work, through their use of 'female' symbolism. Just as Chicago took Georgia O'Keefe's flowers and deemed them vaginal, an evolution of the floral-as-feminine can be found across current practices, such as Amalia Ulman's *MAWU LISA* project:

> MAWU-LISA II is a collective show that showcases and analyses the various visual representations of femininity in today's visual culture. 12 contemporary artists will re-interpret flower paintings, referring to a long tradition of female still-life painters.[26]

Today, if we encounter a work of Amalia Ulman's, such as *Been There* (2010-2012), which contains an assortment of objects that do not depict the artist herself, many of us still read it through the knowledge not only of her opinions and status updates, but of her selfies, of the performative nature of her own identity, and thus we also read the object in these terms – in this case, *performing* 'lower-class aesthetics'. If Chicago is able to make 'social history [...] sit on the plate of an art object', Amalia Ulman does this too by a process of referents.[27] The incorporation of other artists into the project, as well as the femininity imbued in much floral symbolism, present socio-political relations within the art object itself, primarily through performative, *intra-acting* agencies; the multitudinous self appearing and reappearing, not so much as social history, but a form of social analysis. These agencies are derivative of Ulman's social analysis, which occupies her work – work that initially, simply appears as 'pretty things'.

In contrast to Ulman and others such as Cosey Fanni Tutti, Carolee Schneeman and Valie Export, *opposition and refusal* of a certain female representation within the art object has traditionally also been a factor within feminist art practices. Artists such as Nell Tenhaaf and Mary Kelly directly challenge representation. In opposition to the affects manifested in female representations, they directly combated the history of woman's use as object-muse, or the idea of representation as being purely literal/visual. Richard explains that '[a]n initial response from radical feminism is refusal to play the game.'[28] In works such as Kelly's *Post-Partum Document* (1973-77), feminist critique and analysis of identity is advanced via non-bodily representations, which allude instead to all the relational possibilities of representation as being more than skin deep.

Early feminist net.art also challenged 'femininity', through the supposed limits of a text-based internet, some net.art practices engaged in a form of representation that hoped to be posthuman – an identity not limited to a body – and text and code often acted out a disembodied political voice, such as in VNS matrix's cyberfeminist manifesto.

Or in works such as Olia Lialina's interactive stories across web pages, which although using some images, were predominantly text-based narratives that lead the viewer further away from the representation of the artist herself. These net artists' interactions with online as a medium explored it as a non-institutional and separate space – as opposed to one wholly indistinct from the actual, or incited as the institution 2.0, the re-tooled corporation etc. The use of the internet by artists now is far removed from 1997, when Theresa M. Senft wrote:

> I can't see any bodies here, online. Yet words, seemingly attached to bodies in some way, fly past me on this screen. In n-talk (real-time writing) I watch as the cursor key moves back to correct spelling errors of others, transfixed. In the file libraries, there are back-posts from writers who have died. I can read them. This is not to say that the computer defeats death, any more than the library does. Nevertheless, here, in this place that does not defeat death but is itself deathless, that looks like the television and yet is not, where I am playing a part in a drama somewhere, well perhaps not my body, but, nonetheless 'me' – where are the bodies?[29]

JD @jessedarling · Dec 12
Sisters of the nonbinary lower orders its time to admit that gurls in widebrimmed felt hats are the class n gender equiv of dudes in fedoras
Collapse   ↩ Reply ⇄ Retweet ★ Favorited ⋯ More

FAVORITES
5

4:48 PM - 12 Dec 2013 · Details

Reply to @jessedarling

 Molly @mhuzzell · Dec 12
@jessedarling Oh no! fbcdn-sphotos-g-a.akamaihd.net/hphotos-ak-ash… fbcdn-sphotos-a-a.akamaihd.net/hphotos-ak-ash…
Expand   ↩ Reply ⇄ Retweet ★ Favorite ⋯ More

Screenshot from Jesse Darling's Twitter

Quickly, as with all technology, the development of the internet meant that text-based, bodiless, purportedly posthuman identities, not only became image-based, but they also became directly social. Affect and representation hybridised, and this is how I view the feminine aesthetic of today, in 2013.

In difference to hybridisation, Nelly Richard, outlining biopolitical control via the dichotomous masculine/feminine conditions, instead sought transgression in aesthetic spaces, to contradict the terms of what is considered 'female', as a political movement that can operate within art and directly outwards into politics. What exactly is a feminist transgression, is it a posthuman refusal of the gendered and speciated body or, as shown by Richard, the deconstruction of gender through margins that assert its plurality? Or is it the positioning of that which is relegated as feminine, into a neutral, male, space? In this current moment, many women are working towards the problems of representation within art practice, not only by reclaiming agency and using their bodies as art not muse, as many others have done before, but also by looking at the divisions that are part of biopower's constellation. Such divisions include high and low culture, and its intersection with gendering. Feminism's re-callibration of high and low culture has been done by many, namely artists such as Radka Donnell in the 1970s who worked with quilting to examine the non-neutral, feminine *space* as Other and relegated. She pushed to have the feminine *craft* and decorative arts directly penetrate the neutral, male, *fine* art space.

At work throughout the various processes of feminist art are many devices that challenge the patriarchal standards of representation. Not all of them opt for a direct affective occupation of neutral space – some rail for female transgression and deconstruction, while some opt for a complete refusal of gendering, and others call for an overturning and reconfiguration of the (gendered) hierarchies within aesthetics and culture itself. Nevertheless, they are all acutely aware of the structures of representation and seek to disarm them by opening up a gap within assumed 'neutrality'. For Richard, a rejection or transgression of femininity is what is required to undo the spatial neutrality that prescribes binaries such as masculine or feminine, and she asks, '[h]ow can feminist criticism be a *deterritorialising* force?' Yet we have lived through the neoliberal subsumption of all 'other' identities into the homogeneous singular identity of the consumer commodity. Richard's spatial idea of oppression via neutrality is very important, and her demands still hold some weight, yet the process needs to be a reformulated attack on neutral territory, it cannot come through deconstruction of identity alone.

This is where affect and feminine aesthetics are tricky because they sit most clearly within identity yet, through their embeddedness and self-distribution, some are undoubtedly beginning to perform in an actively political way within the neutral order itself. They often use many differing and perhaps oppositional devices, and the reification of affect is of course, at first glance, the 'relation between people [that] takes on the character of a thing and thus acquires a "phantom objectivity".[30] Within this reification of our relations the question is whether or not we maintain Massumi's *primacy of affect?* If affective labour is the unpaid, invisible process that facilitates female oppression, could a certain reification of affect bring this process to light, whilst at the same time deviating from a more hierarchical (or 'neutral') commodity form, and resisting parody? For Massumi, image-reception is performed on many levels, and viewing this as reified and spectral is important when considering the functions of affective self-branding and multi-platform distribution that these artists employ, '(f)or depending on which is the case, all the subjective phenomena in the societies concerned are objectified in qualitatively different ways.'[31]

Bunny Rogers – A Case Study

Bunny Rogers is a characteristic example of an artist who has recently been slammed for involving her self-image/persona in her work.[32] The work extends across her social media presence, yet instead of simply collapsing the mediation of the self, this builds, as with Ulman and others, into a narrative that can be read through art objects, often via the artists' social media sites. This reflexivity thus begins to build a critique of a demonstrated condition of self within society – the relational and performative refract into each other attacking, making up, and trying to repurpose some sort of new conversation that captivates others; a potentially active self/social awareness.

Rogers' practice mixes sculpture, craft and web page pieces. In terms of the re-mixing of feminist practices into a 'feminine aesthetic', this is further developed by the instant opportunity to create identity and distribute self-representation across networks, often shining a light onto the female condition, with a knowing affirmation of its familiarity: 'He wants a family. But with me?'[33] Rogers' work takes the female gender as it applies to her self, her own affective experience and rebuilds it into something uncanny, referencing outside stories or spaces, beyond what can be contained in

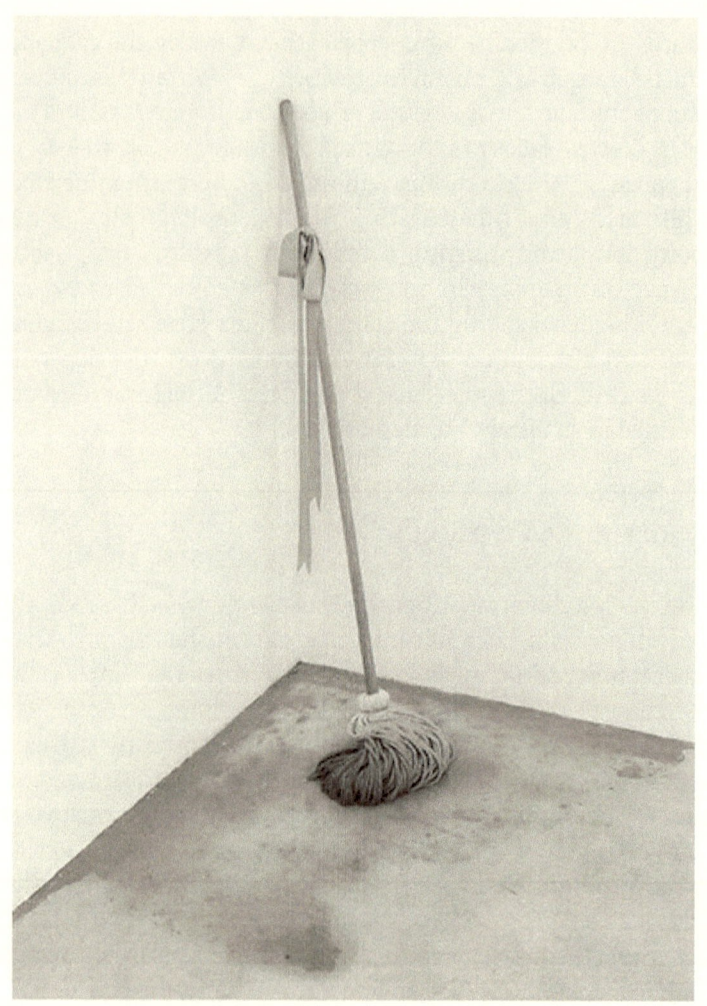

Bunny Rogers, *Self portrait (mourning mop)*, 2013

her social media presence alone. In one of Rogers' anthropomorphised sculptures, *Self Portrait (mourning mop)*, 2013, the one solitary bow reminds us of the practices of many artists, particularly in the 1970s – like those of Faith Ringgold and Miriam Schapiro – who reclaimed craft materials and motifs of womanhood for making contemporary fine art objects. In *mourning mop*, the lineage of self-portraiture as a male pastime, the ego-sanctioned self-image (which is not gendered), is put into question by Rogers' distinct decision to remove her self-image from the self-portrait. The way it really works is in its reproductive qualities – affect splinters into the gaps in your own experience, over and over again. Every time you look at a mop afterwards, you are reminded of Rogers' self-portrait, and its non-literal self-representation that silently screams, domestic, cornered object.

Bunny's poignant reflection on the human condition, her diversion of personal experience into artworks, also spans different media. In Rogers' *9Years*, she documents her individual avatar's journeys in Second Life in a photographic series (2009-ongoing). *9Years* is a bleak and critical expression of the subjugation of women, and the loneliness felt whilst seeking interaction, some touch, some acceptance and social recognition. The disturbing awkwardness of angles, the *Uncanny Valley*-esque sentiment that renders the awkward avatar, Bunny Winterwolf, a ghost-like half human, shows the explicit and literal scenarios experienced by Rogers in Second Life. The work shows someone's hands holding her down, or Winterwolf's body in compromisingly different outfits and positions, forcing its girl self into hopeful acceptability, wandering in the landscape of Second Life sex rooms and topographies that speak of a distorted wilderness and of Winterwolf's feelings on her travels. As put by Donna Haraway, 'There are no pre-constituted subjects and objects, and no single sources, unitary actors, or final ends. In Judith Butler's terms, there are only "contingent foundations"; bodies that matter are the result.'[34] For me this exactly summarises Rogers' approach, or even, medium – refusing universalism in favour of more explicitly utilising Barad's intra-acting agencies for the creation of a (non-neutral) art object. Rogers' has stated 'I see a lot of overlap in mass culture's sexualization and exploitation of children and animals.'[35] It is perhaps no coincidence then that this Haraway quote comes from *The Companion Species Manifesto*. For Haraway and Rogers, the object-subject / human-non-human is privy to the same long-term culturing, hierarchical power structuring, and exploitation; stated from different starting points, and even intent. For both there lies a similar way of thinking, of creating a holistic practice in which to inject subjectivity and politics into a single (object) work.

Gap, Affect

The work by the artists most discussed in this text – Rogers, Ulman and White – uses representation inflected with personal narrative, registering and generating affect not only in their artworks and their vivid titles, but also through their online presence – 'my pain is better than yours' (Ulman).[36] Coming to their own practice as already immanent and immersed in biopower, they attempt to charge it with a practice that is disseminated across agents. Knowing the lineage and variation of feminist art practices, its insertion of the neutral and generic representation of the female condition, and even 'femininity', we begin to think beyond the positioning of self-representation in feminist art, and instead reflect upon the status of affect and the gaps created by it. Lauren Berlant articulates the complex psychological relationship between a state of subjection and its potential overcoming: '[c]ruel optimism is the condition of maintaining an attachment to a problematic object in *advance* of its loss.'[37] We need to begin to locate these gaps, rather than what is represented, as a viable mode of feminist art practice. Is a *Lonely Girl* only replicating the image of women patriarchy prescribes? Or is this image also achieved through female self-representation itself, thus opening a space where the demands of prescription can be critiqued?[38]

Of course raising an issue can be productive, yet there is a need for art to be actively productive. As Archey points out, when a slew of female selfies used to advertise an all-female line up of an art show is organised by a man, it casts the whole process of self-representation into question.[39] How fragile, or at risk, are feminine aesthetics within the same biopolitical society they critique.

I would like to repurpose Nick Srniecek's ideas on mediation between the aesthetic sublime and the aesthetics of the interface, in relation to Brain Massumi's proposition of affectivity's primacy within in-between space. In *Navigating Neoliberalism*, Srnicek outlines the need for the left to be able to use what Jameson refers to as 'cognitive mapping', in order both to navigate the systems of capitalism as an ideological and economic structure of the biopowerful everyday, of agential realism, and to place the human within this. To reflect on the experience of our technological climate, whilst also using technologies to map an outline of the systems which construct our lives. The aesthetics of the interface are suggested as a way of counteracting our inability to cognitively map the complex realities we live in today, and the relationship of the two forming a space where we may be able to propose

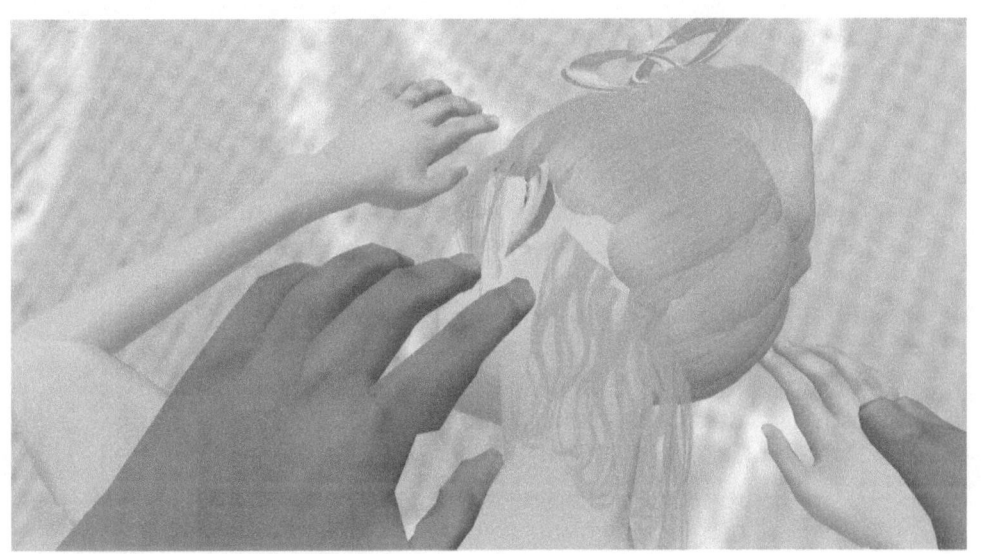
Bunny Rogers, *9Years*, photo series, 2009 – ongoing

a non-dystopian future. One that offers an alternative to a present reality of knowing collapse, demonstrated across society – corporations and banks are refusing to lend, 'even capitalist realism has lost a sense of the future.'[40]

The feminine aesthetic – of mediation between the biopolitical sublime and the social media interface, or its cognitive mapping, is an in-between space of affect, as demonstrated by Holly White. The affective gap, between subject position and proposed alternatives (Holly White 'looking for you', in a non-era specific 'topia of sorts) is almost a material proxy of reflexivity, yet goes further and imagines a future after capitalist realism, using neutrality as a spatial construct. If the primacy of the affective is marked by the gap between content and effect, it would appear that the strength or duration of an image's effect is not logically connected to the content in any straightforward way. This is not to say that there is no connection and no logic, but that affect-in-action is predicated on *intra-action*, movements, and feminine aesthetics de-neutralising force; occupying neutral territory, in slight opposition to Richard's call to 'de-territorialize', calling for action, not refusal. The primacy of affect is embodied in the spectral form, of sub-fractured new subjectivities sprawled out across the network.

If we allow for a transgression of the *cruel optimism* that our affective desires are pinned to, instead allowing our affective demands to take position amongst the neutral, we can drive the 'physically impossible but vitalizing movement of rhetorical animation that permits subjects to suspend themselves in the optimism of a potential occupation of the same psychic space of others.'[41] We can use the spectral commodity form that is cruel optimism as a means to pit desire and affect against neutral, normative structures that sure up oppression.

I hope for greater structural transgression to spill out of the position of immanence-within-the individual that it currently falls within. This is why, continuing to direct feminine aesthetics into political discourse and challenges, the process of mapping pluralities of Others and demanding that structure itself be transgressive, does to an extent refuse neutrality. The aim of penetrating space, in a progression whose future would be one of de-territorialisation, as demanded by Richard, *is* being done without deconstruction, and more so by continually confronting and affronting the neutral. 'Aesthetics is politics', and feminine aesthetics are un-neutral aesthetics by default.[42] If we can resist neutrality in itself, then we are in effect resisting patriarchy, what follows from the un-neutral is both the feminine, and everything else (that isn't neutral). We cannot rest at the cruelly optimistic moment the affective adheres to.

Footnotes

1 Mermaid Cunt (http://mermaidcunt.tumblr.com/) and Queer Libido (http://queerlibido.tumblr.com/) are Tumblrs that speak their own position as radical subjectivities, yet Tumblr is a perfect example of the way in which 'free speech' for these subjectivities is explicitly embedded in capitalism: the corporation Yahoo owns the blog platform Tumblr.
2 I am, for this text, determining feminine aesthetics as artist practices which use affect as material, due to the gendering of affect. I would need many more words to unpack the term 'feminine aesthetics' in terms of visual features such as 'the colour pink', and so on. I am also exploring feminine aesthetics as a type of organisation after networks, which refuses neutrality (as a structural enforcement of gendered hierarchies), and perhaps could also be described as 'Un-Neutral Aesthetics' – via the occupation of patriarchal space by an explicitly non-male gender.
3 Jodi Dean, 'Communicative Capitalism: Circulation and the Foreclosure of Politics', *Cultural Politics*, 2005, Vol.1, Issue 1, pp.51-74.
4 Nick Srnircek, 'Navigating Neoliberalism: Political Aesthetics in an Age of Crisis', presented at The Matter of Contradiction: Ungrounding the Object, France, 8-9 September 2012.
5 'Pure Immanence' as laid out by Gilles Deleuze is seen within a *plane of immanence* – a complete embeddedness that denies transcendence as distinct from immanence. Pure immanence is thus often referred to as a pure plane, an infinite field or smooth space without substantial or constitutive division: 'It is only when immanence is no longer immanence to anything other than itself that we can speak of a plane of immanence.' Gilles Deleuze, *Pure Immanence: Essays on A Life*, New York: Zone Books, 2001, p.27.
6 See Hakim Bey, T.A.Z. *The Temporary Autonomous Zone: Ontological Anarchy*, Autonomedia, 1991, http://hermetic.com/bey/taz_cont.html
7 After Marx, the concept was developed extensively by Georg Lukács, in particular in the essay 'Reification and the Consciousness of the Proletariat', in *History and Class Consciousness*, UK: The Merlin Press, 1971, pp.83-222.
8 'Intra-acting agencies' is the process of relations in the ontological state of *Agential Realism* – a theory devised by feminist and physics theorist Karen Barad. See: 'Agential Realism: Feminist Interventions in Understanding Scientific Practices' in *The Science Studies Reader*, Mario Biagioli, (ed.), 1998, and 'Posthumanist Performativity: Toward an Understanding of How Matter Comes to Matter', in *Signs*, Vol.28 No.3, 2003, pp.801-831.
9 From the press release for Johann Arens' exhibition, Internet Centre & Habesh Grocery, at Paradise Row Gallery, 13 December 2013-1 February 2014, London, http://www.paradiserow.com/exhibitions/98/overview/
10 Nick Snircek, ibid.
11 See Katja Diefenbach, 'The Spectral Form of Value: Ghost-Things and Relations of Forces', Zach Formwalt (trans.), European Institute for Progressive Cultural Policies, 2006, http://eipcp.net/transversal/1106/diefenbach/en
12 Lauren Berlant, 'Cruel Optimism', *The Affect Theory Reader*, USA: Duke University Press, 2010, pp.93-117.

13 Holly White, *I'm on my bike because I'm looking for you*, 2013, http://www.youtube.com/watch?v=1mAd77WAwdk
14 *Immaterial Labor*, Maurizio Lazzarato, 1996, https://wiki.brown.edu/confluence/download/attachments/73535007/lazzarto-immaterial+labor.pdf (accessed 21/02/13)
15 Karen Barad, op. cit.
16 Brian Massumi, *Autonomy of Affect*, 1995, http://www.brianmassumi.com/textes/Autonomy%20of%20Affect.PDF (accessed 14/06/13)
17 Lauren Berlant, op. cit.
18 Ibid.
19 See Corinna Kirsch, 'The Digital Art World's (Secret) Feminism', *Art F City*, October 2013, http://artfcity.com/2013/10/04/the-digital-art-worlds-secret-feminism/
20 Amy Knight, in an interview with Darja Bajagi, *Symbol*, Issue 4, 2013.
21 Ibid.
22 dward Soja's concept of *Thirdspace* is a real and imagined spatial condition where subjectivity and objectivity converge, into a landscape of transdiciplinary everyday life, unending history – viewing human life as spatial and part of the fabric of this space. See Edward Soja, *Thirdspace: Journeys to Los Angeles and Other Real-and-Imagined Places*, Blackwell, 2000.
23 See Elvia Wilk, 'Where Looks Don't Matter and Only the Best Writers Get Laid', *Cluster Mag*, Party Issue 2013, http://theclustermag.com/t2013/05/feminism-and-other-unfulfilled-promises-of-the-text-based-internet/
24 Nelly Richard, *Masculine/Feminine: Practices of Difference*, USA: Duke University Press, 2004, p.10.
25 bid.
26 Amalia Ulman, from Mawu Lisa website: http://mawu-lisa.com/
27 Jane Gerhard, *The Dinner Party: Judy Chicago and the Power of Popular Feminism, 1970-2007*, USA: University of Georgia, 2013, p.2.
28 Nelly Richard, op. cit., p.12.
29 See Theresa M. Senft, 'Spare Parts', first published in *The End(s) of Performance*, New York University, 1997. http://www.terrisenft.net/writing/spareparts.html
30 Georg Lukács, written 1923, http://www.marxists.org/archive/lukacs/works/history/hcc05.htm
31 Ibid.
32 See Sarah Nicole Prickett's, 'Sein und Zit', *Artforum*, October 2013, http://artforum.com/slant/section=slant&archive=201310 . When reading this, I was affronted by the hypocrisy of its tone and direction in regard to the history of the male-artist persona, and the use of this persona in artists' careers (without this being seen as a ghettoising or gendering of their practice).
33 Status update from Bunny Rogers' Facebook, see also her poetry blog, http://cunny4.tumblr.com/
34 Donna Haraway, *The Companion Species Manifesto*, Prickly Paradigm Press, 2003, p.6.
35 Bunny Rogers Artist Profile, Louis Doulas, May 2012, http://rhizome.org/editorial/2012/may/15/artist-profile-bunny-rogers/ (accessed 07/11/13).
36 Amalia Ulman Facebook update.
37 Lauren Berlant, op. cit., p.94.
38 Lonely Girl was a controversial, all female exhibition (curated by a man), at Martos Gallery, New York. See Karen Archey's review in *Frieze*, issue 159: http://www.frieze.com/issue/review/lonely-girl/

39 Ibid.
40 Nick Snircek, op. cit.
41 Lauren Berlant, op. cit., p.95.
42 Jacques Rancière, *The Politics of Aesthetics*, UK: Continuum, 2007.

MOVEMENTS OF SAFETY, A SAFETY MOVEMENT, SAFETY IN MOVEMENT

MICHA CÁRDENAS

From a Free Software Movement to a Free Safety Movement

This essay is a call to all feminist hackers, anti-racist coders, gender hackers, genderchangers, queer and trans hackers, political hackers, dancers, movement makers, poets, performers, anti-violence activists and networked activists to come together to help stop violence against queer and trans* people, people of colour, disabled people and women. Many forms of daily violence – sexual, gender, racial, ableist and state-sponsored – are only increasing. As global warming, neoliberalism and neocolonialism continue, more and more people are subject to violence on a daily basis due to social instability. This is a call to people to acknowledge that the internet era has not brought more safety but less. This is a call to say we need more people hacking safety, where hacking involves a creative use of the imagination to solve a problem. Why do we have better software to share pictures of lunch than we do to keep each other safe?

These solutions can take all forms, from technological to social ones to combinations of the two. To think about ending violence with technology we need to think broadly about what violence means and what technology is: movement is a technology, gender is a technology, language is a technology, code is a technology. We need more collaboration between hackers, activists and artists to end violence. We need networked devices which people can use to call on their personal networks for help, games to teach people not to rape, mechanisms for bystanders to step in and stop violence, discrete ways for people in private situations to call for help when violence occurs in their homes.

I started the project Local Autonomy Networks two years ago to create wearable electronics to prevent sexual and gender violence against queer and trans* people of colour. In those two years I have made prototypes of devices including dresses, hoodies and bracelets which have wireless transmitters in them and can be used to call for help. Some of these devices can detect the proximity of other devices. I have been working towards adding GPS units so that the call for help can be accompanied with a location. But, I am only one person. This problem is much much bigger than me.

I am an artist, hacker, activist, writer. I am not a business person or an engineer. I have spent much of the last two years doing workshops and performances with people in different cities to build the social agreements necessary for us to keep each other safe in a world where police often cause more violence, if they even show up. In some of the cities I work in people have told me repeatedly that they would not call the police because they

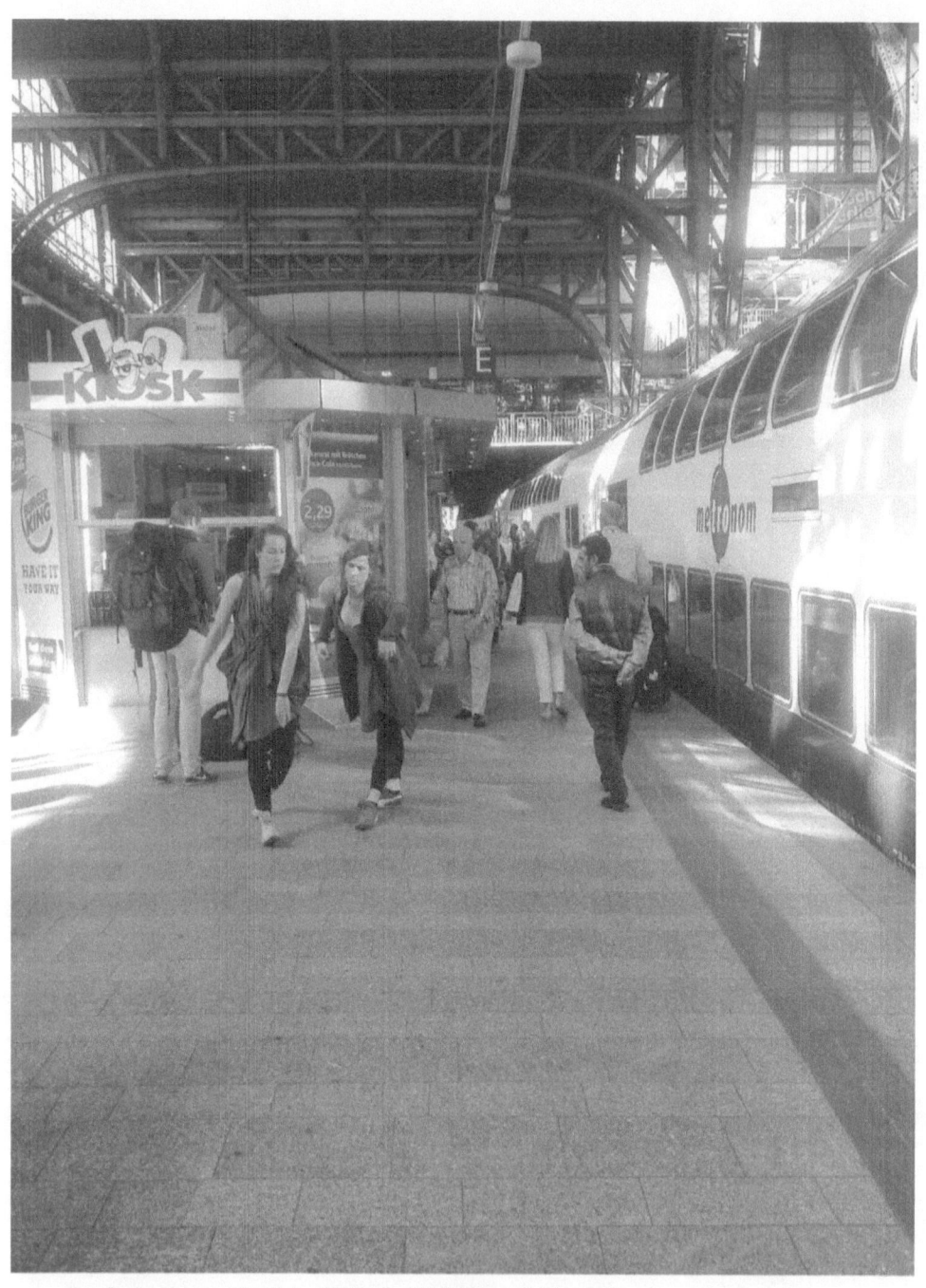

Performance with Micha Cárdenas, NM Rosen and Tikul in Hamburg Hauptbahnhof.
Photos by Zach Blas. 2013

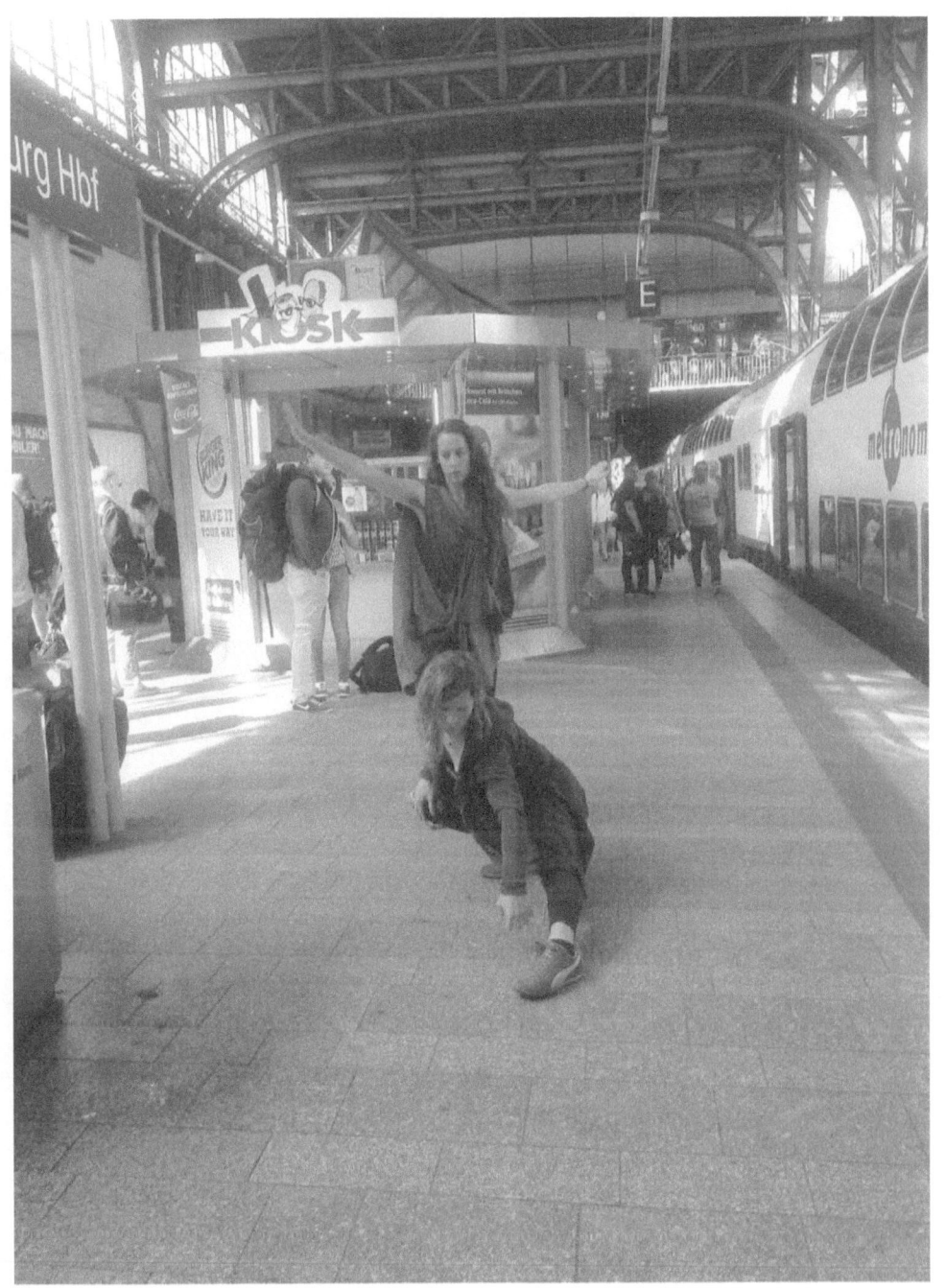

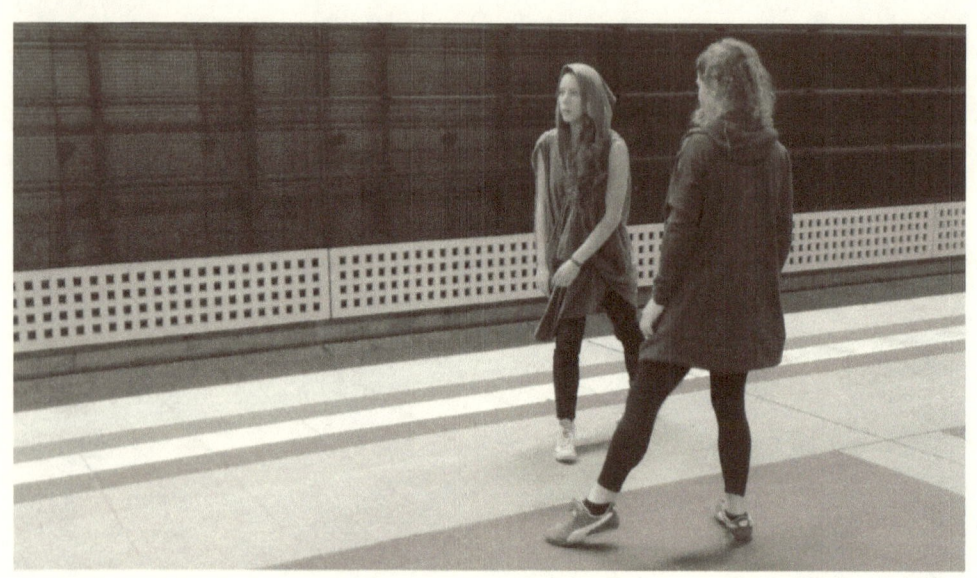
Performance with Micha Cárdenas, NM Rosen and Tikul in Berlin Hauptbahnhof.
Photos by Zach Blas, 2013

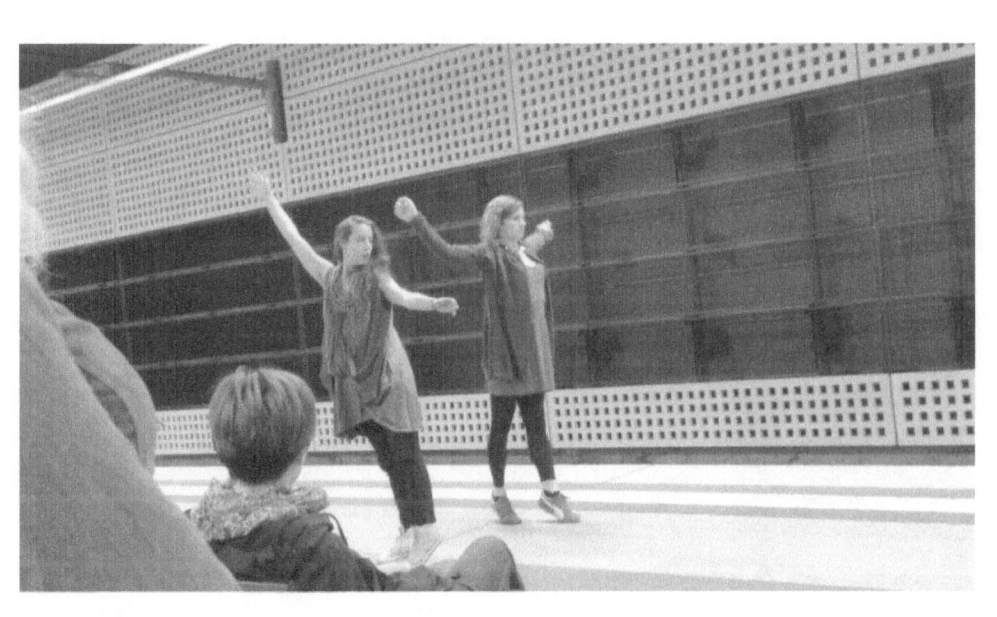

won't ever show up. Anti-violence activists have also told me that it is common that queer and trans* people and people of colour know not to call the police because they inflict more violence in most cases.

I have shifted my role in this project from building electronics to building the infrastructure for a network of networks, for people to be able to contribute and think together and discuss this problem together. Lots of people. The free software movement has been incredibly successful since it began 30 years ago. What we need now is a movement for free safety, a movement of people who want to figure out how to make transformative justice happen in increasingly networked societies, a movement that will develop networks for safety that don't rely on the corporations and police that daily perpetrate violence on our communities, a movement of people who will agree to keep each other safe from unjust forms of violence.

This needs to happen in a distributed way, and can't depend on me. Everywhere I have gone in the past two years throughout the Americas and in Europe, people have told me: we need this here. Violence is a problem that exists everywhere and is getting worse. So please join me and help build this movement and send me and everyone else an email. Or tweet about it. Or Facebook about it. There are many ways of using existing technologies such as Circle Of 6, Foursquare and Group Me for safety.

What is important is that solutions need to be affordable. There is already a huge industry of safety products and if safety is something that only certain people can afford and clearly that is an unjust situation. So we must make these solutions affordable.

What is also crucial in this movement is to develop safety solutions that maintain people's privacy. Solutions which can be exploited by law enforcement to surveille people do not make them more safe but less.

What is most important to me in this movement is to centralise the needs of the most affected groups of people: transgender women of colour are the number one targets of hate crimes, sex workers are often subject to violence, and disabled people are also subject to violence on a daily basis and can benefit uniquely from networks of communication and support.

I have set up a web page at http://autonets.org/movement to continue this conversation and share detailed documentation of the prototypes I have made and the workshops I have facilitated. This is a call for you to take up this project in your own city, talk to others about how to build networks, technological or otherwise, of safety and support for survivors of violence. What follows is a description of one local project which engages with technologies of inter-urban transportation networks to develop strategies for safety in Germany.

The Safe Itinerant / The Insecurity of Mobility // Der sichere Wanderer / Die Gefahren von Mobilität

We are safe when we walk.
We have walked for generations.
Your colonial regimes want to stop us, name and identify us.
We won't be stopped by your policing violence,
We won't be named by your regimes.

Autonets Berlin / Lüneburg – The Safe Itinerant / The Insecurity of Mobility // Der sichere Wanderer / Die Gefahren von Mobilität took place in sites spanning Berlin, Hamburg and Lüneburg, created by myself in collaboration with the Post-Media Lab, Zach Blas, Tikul and N.M. Rosen. Starting with a performance at Berlin Hauptbahnhof, platform 7 at 11:30AM, the mobile performance and seminar continued with a performance in the Hamburg Hauptbahnhof, a mobile seminar on the Deutschebahn trains to Lüneberg and concluded with a discussion with local scholars at the Post-Media Lab at Leuphana University at 15:45.

From Oscar Grant, a black man killed in San Francisco at a public train station by private train police, to the 2012 sexual assault of a woman by a group of men on a bus in New Delhi, India, to the attack of CeCe McDonald while walking with friends, to the murder of Trayvon Martin while walking home, the promises of urban mobility are repeatedly belied by the violence that is used to police spaces of transit and the ways that access to mobility is regulated. This mobile performance/seminar considered the themes of mobility, violence and access, using the actual space of transit, the train and train station, as the space of performance, discussion and presentation. The performance is part of the project *Local Autonomy Networks*, which works towards networks of community-based responses to violence through performance and dance. This part of the series considered how translocal networks of safety can be imagined within spaces which are intensely regulated yet fall between the lines of local regulations. Engaging with the Post-Media Lab's theme of Organisation After Networks, this performance considered how communities can organise for safety after their lives have been shaped by inter-urban and transnational transportation networks.

In the seminars, we discussed the following themes:

- The cloud versus a home / colonial dream of mobility versus decolonial construction

- Safety in numbers / gendering of public space
- The itinerant scholar / the safe itinerant / the itinerant artist
- The insecurity of mobility / gender/sexuality/race in transit and across borders
- From passport checks to biometric mobility controls
- Ticketing systems / e-ticketing
- The price of speed / the cost of easy border crossing
- Mobile public space / from public to corporate transit / public interstitial space
- The promise of mobility / disability and access

The movement piece was based on a choreographic score that came from actual safety strategies we have had to use in train stations in Berlin. In the first part of the score one dancer would get in between the other dancer and the audience, to protect them from the audience and allow them to move however they wanted, to make the act of holding space and solidarity against violence visible. In the second part, the roles of protector and protected switched. In the third part, we protected each other, imagining our backs to be a shield and protecting the space in between us.

One of the many embodied discoveries of the day, which we discussed in our final seminar at the Post Media Lab, was the differences between inter-urban transportation networks and intra-urban transportation networks. While our experience in Berlin was that subway trains within the city were a frequent site of gendered, racialized and homophobic violence, the experience on trains between cities was very different. Deutsche Bahn (DB) creates a much more regulated zone for immigration controls, checking each traveler's passport and credit card on trains between cities, for example. Additionally, the high cost of travel between cities on DB trains creates a class segregated space. As such, the space of DB trains and train stations was a much safer space for performance and discussion than a U-Bahn train through the city of Berlin, but only because all of the participants in the performance and seminar had legal immigration or visitor status in Germany and financial support from institutions to facilitate the performance. This reveals the need for community based methods of preventing violence in mobile sites such as DB and U-Bahn trains which can provide safety both for queer and trans people of colour as well as for undocumented migrants. Additionally, there is a need for strategies that can provide this protection from state violence, such as immigration control, in order to allow more autonomy of movement for people who do not have legal immigration status.

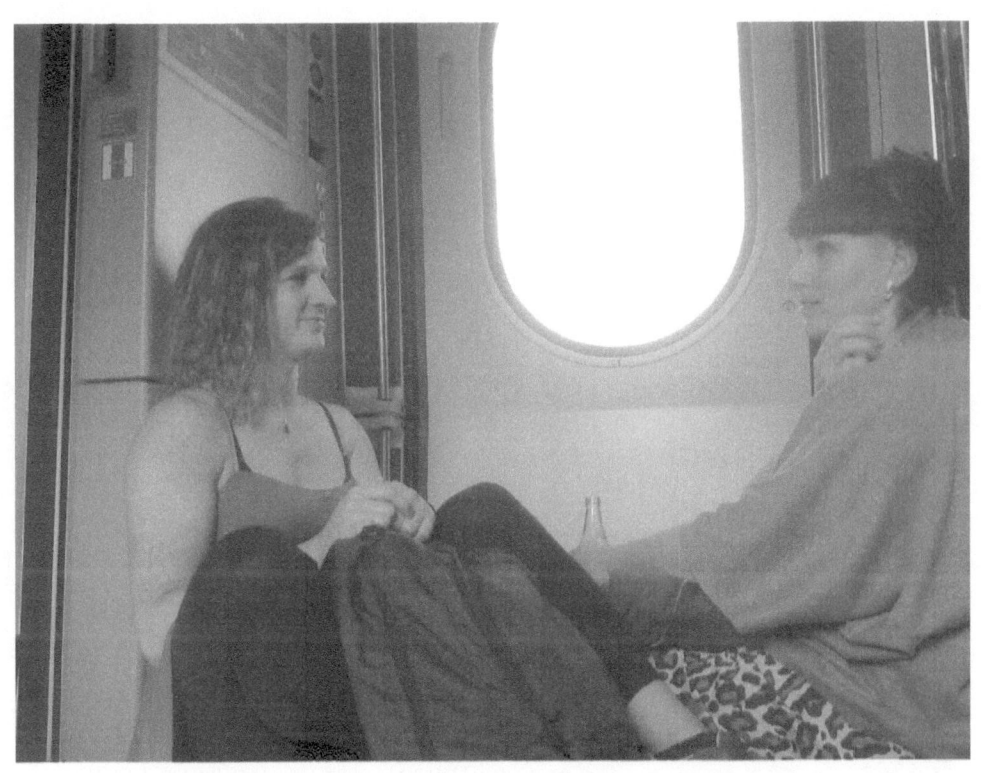

Mobile seminar on the Deutsche Bahn train to *Lüneburg*. Photo by Micha Cárdenas, 2013

At our last seminar of the day in the Post Media Lab, a participant joined our discussion who was pregnant. She brought another level of precarity into our considerations. Her presence demonstrated the current ways that communities daily provide safety for members of a community that are precarious because of a shared value, childrearing. She also pointed to the need to further develop our structures of safety for future needs that are yet unimagined or unborn.

CLICK SOCIAL ACTIVISM? A LOCALISATION OF POLITICAL PARTICIPATION AFTER NETWORKS

MORITZ QUEISNER

The Arena of Protest

The practices of the Occupy movement have reintroduced the category of space into forms of political protest. While the logistics of Occupy are built substantially upon digital networks, it was the physical assembly within squares and camps that made it a movement. The organisational logic of Occupy bridged the gap between online and offline protest by moving political participation from the internet to the streets. It was precisely this spatial shift of self-organised networks that triggered artist and activist collective Free Art and Technology Lab's idea for the browser extension Occupy the Internet! By occupying any website with virtual protesters, the armchair activist would still be able to participate 'in the recent global wave of revolution from the comfort of [her or his] home computer.'[1] At first glance this sounds like an obvious critique of online protest, but the virtual occupation of Zuccotti Park on Google Maps for instance instead points to the fact that the practices of online and offline protest are increasingly converging.

A key and widely contested argument in the current debate about the transformation of activism and protest, which Occupy the Internet! has emerged from, relates to the spatial mobilisation of location-bound practices: political participation in the digital society may no longer need the physical assembly of its actors. The networked technology paradigm has apparently detached communication from bodily presence. The main characteristic of this post-medial crisis is the transformation of individual forms of interaction. Net culture, has enabled new kinds of social interaction and community based forms of communication typically described as 'participatory' or 'democratic' – a concept that we tend to call 'social media'. Social media has created a dialogic and rhizomatic media culture that diverges from the atomistic communication infrastructure of the 20th century. The one-sided separation between broadcasters and recipients has been replaced or at least significantly extended, by a shared and horizontal feedback infrastructure whose participants are permanently broadcasting.

This transformation of communication goes along with a transformation of political participation that can be described by distinguishing three levels: actor, action and place. The first two have continuously dominated political debates about digital media: on an actor-level it is especially the empowerment of the individual that has initiated a new form of political agents such as followers, whistle-blowers, crowd-funders, bloggers or hacktivists – hardly very distinct classifications. Those actors have

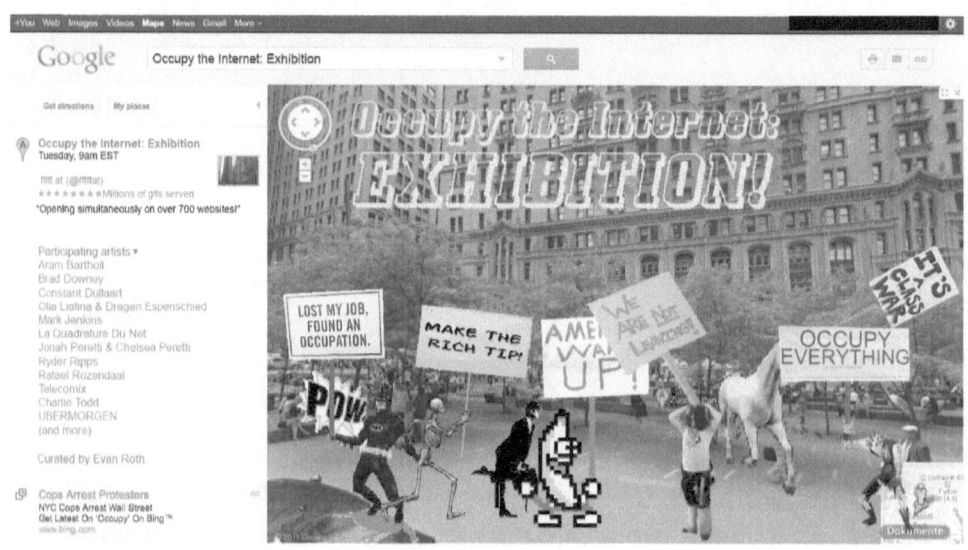

Evan Roth & Free Art and Technology Lab, animated gif still of the Occupy the Internet! exhibition flyer, 2012

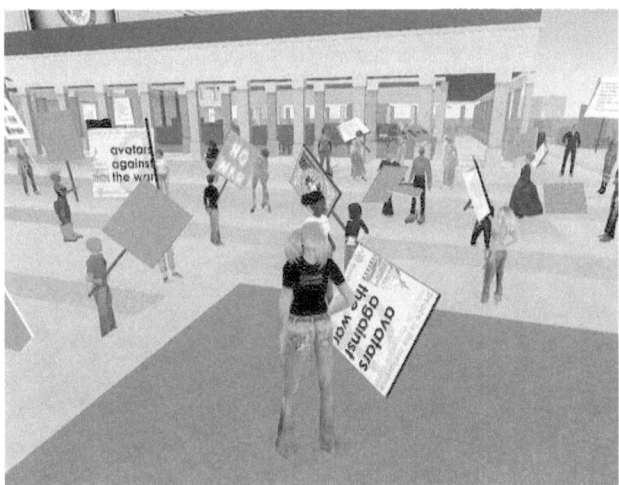

Screenshot of the 'avatars against the war' demonstration, Second Life, 2007

established new forms of action, whose central element of political power is accessing and exchanging information and whose types of interaction are neither hierarchic, centralised or institutionalised nor limited by spatial relations, territorial regulation or individual ownership. In other words, they do not necessarily depend on location (e.g. filesharing, DoS-attacks, crowdsourcing, liking, data mining, following etc.)

The idea behind this paper is in contrast to this image of activism, to reconsider the category of place for the forms of political participation. The assumption is that there is a correlation between the transformation of social interaction and the current turn of the notion of place through location based media. It argues against the tendency that the relevance of place seems to have vanished with the ubiquity of digital computing. In the following three sections I would like to suggest that territoriality becomes increasingly important for the configuration of political action by developing a brief media history of the place in order to localise the changing forms of participation.

Space – the Final Frontier

On the morning of October 12th 1492 Christoph Columbus occupied America by plunging his banner deep into the sandy ground of the Bahamas. If we compare Columbus' occupation to the contemporary Occupy movement,

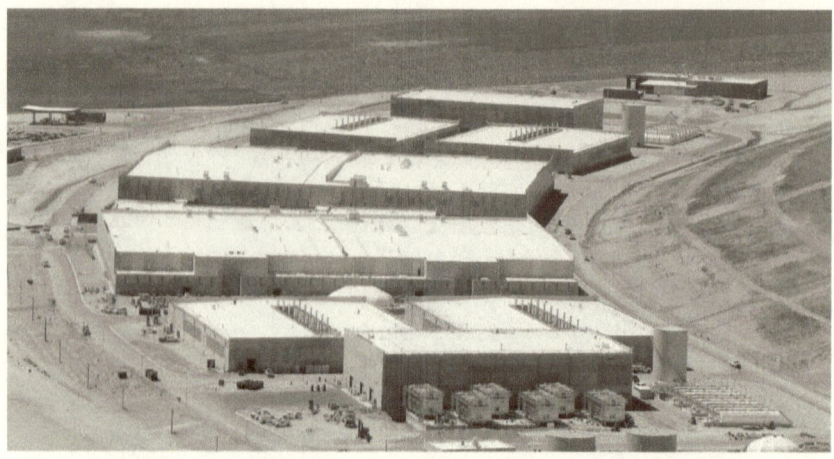

NSA Utah Data Centre, United States, The Domestic Surveillance Directorate, 2013

both forms of political practice are profoundly based on the category of place, where people claim a collective interest. The borders of what seems possible, of what seemed reachable to us, have long been dependent on spatial categories: on the movement of ourselves. Even science fiction narratives have mostly drawn on the notion of transit spaces in order to extend the 'final frontier' in order to 'explore strange new worlds, to seek out new life and new civilizations, to boldly go where no man has gone before' (Star Trek). When jumping into hyperspace, territory is no discrete abstract entity but an extended physical space, that corresponds much more to a vague than a virtual expansion of space. While this experience of space traditionally lays within the physical dimensions of the human body, this idea has been fundamentally challenged by electronic communication and later by digital media.

The anthropological organisation of space fell into crisis was when people were able to move information faster than themselves, when spatial thinking became emancipated from bodily presence. A phenomenon that we still euphorically refer to as the information revolution. Among the shades of this revolution, postmodern media theory largely neglected the concept of place. In the network society, information is rather described as a constant flow such as timelines or livestreams. In media theory this relativisation of anthropological boundaries of communication has lead to paradigms such as 'the end of geography' (Jean Baudrillard), 'the elimination of space' (Paul Virilio) or the 'disappearance of distance' (Vilém Flusser).[2] Until today this concept has been connected to the vision of a network society in which the question of place appeared to have vanished: the relative position of places to each other has been trivialised by spatial and temporal compression. The innovations of the so-called web 2.0 and ubiquitous computing have instead been accompanied by a topos that separates spatial movement from the human body – the everywhere of the 'global village' corresponds to an 'esthétique de la disparition' to quote the two most canonical terms from Marshall McLuhan and Virilio.

Arguing against the idea of this everywhere-ideology, the Occupy movement has given us a reason to localise the arena of online protest. The movement has shown that political actors of a digital society do not simply consist of virtual masses of protesting avatars, slacktivists or followers and that their actions do not only involve likes, DoS attacks, tweets, virtual demonstrations or one-click donations. But that the development from the isolated mass media spectator to the post-media networker of tactical technology integrates virtual and real forms of political participation. Accordingly, the assumption is that the forms of political protest dissociate from the concept of the virtual, while our interaction with and through digital technology becomes increasingly socially integrated and spatially contingent.

Cyberspace and the Information Superhighway

The rise of digital media did finally put an end to the limit of the traditional narration of space that culminated in the metaphor of cyberspace – a term that still represents the idea of the virtual as a parallel space whose only border is its difference from the physical. Most attempts to represent spatial relations beyond the physical have depicted the virtual either as an undefined space or as a tool of transmission. Perhaps you remember those awkward visualisations of the so-called information superhighway from the 1990s: deep blue data streets or dark tunnels towards a nowhere consisting of ones and zeros. Those visualisations of the web corresponded to an imagination of political participation styled upon the *Matrix* – either you were in or out.

Back then the World Wide Web was first and foremost imagined as a non-place: it was rather a highway than a square. Even though protest within the virtual could be spatially related, it remained an isolated and autonomous space, disconnected from any notion of place – a second life, that transcended our first lives. This 'dualism', as Sherry Turkle framed it,

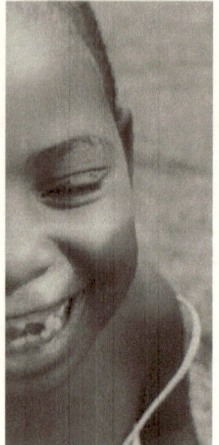

One-click charity, advertisement on Amazon.com, 2013

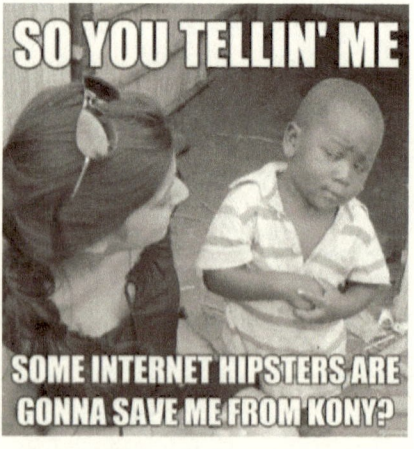

Meme relating to the 'Stop Kony' campaign of Invisible Children Inc., anonymous, 2012

or this 'delusion' to quote Evgeny Morozov, still shapes our view and the critique of the forms of political participation after the social web – about 20 years after the cyberhype.[3] A central quality of the social web is that it enables users to share content almost independent from spatial boundaries but still in real-time, for instance by organising political protest via Packet Radio, SMS or Twitter, by live-streaming what happens on the streets or through integrated community media like delegative or liquid democracy.

Those practices have created an architecture of participation which distinguishes them from the physical assembly of the parliament or the demonstration. An architecture that enables new forms of participation and intervention into political processes but that has also brought new places into the spotlight. Places such as the world's largest archive of political activism in Utah, United States, operated by the United States National Security Agency (NSA). Or Facebook's new server farm in Lulea, Finland close to the arctic circle where most of our Western European Facebook data is stored and processed. Both sites are still far from being in the centre of any political action, but they represent what I would call a shift in the organisational logic of the social web. They show that data is not free-floating in space, but that it is physical infrastructure that moves data – mostly fibre optic cables in the ground which are owned by corporations. And, even more importantly, they point to the fact that every single bit has an exact geolocation at any given time. This stands in opposition to the vision of an omnipresent, pervasive and ubiquitous digital space, that shapes the imagination of online protest as a form of political action in which information is not just simultaneously available (in time), but also also everywhere (in space).

Accordingly, we can observe the formation of a horizontal and decentralised infrastructure of complex networks, in which digital media mobilises and organises a new form of political power. I signed a petition with Avaaz for global justice, I donated a dollar of my Amazon special deal coupon to feed a child in Mali, I denial-of-service attacked the Bank of America from my backyard, I liked a website against Nazis, I down-voted a racist comment on Youtube etc. The world wide debate around the Kony 2012 campaign about child soldiers in Uganda has shown that there is an increasing awareness that the social web does not simply virtualise the places of the political, but fosters a re-negotiation of what we want the places of political participation to be like. Millions of memes depict this gap between participation and location, between the virtual and the physical.

Hybrid Space and Location Awareness

While at first glance the forms of political participation in the era of the social web seem to become increasingly detached from places, we can also identify a shift, that pinpoints the limits of deterritorialisation – an idea that Aram Bartholl's work, *Map* (2006), addresses by transcribing the icons of the web into forms outside of the digital. This kind of limitation of ubiquitous computing became visible when the restrictions of connectivity within the Arab Spring forced protesters to use traditional place-bound media such as fax messages, leaflets, landlines or word of mouth. The shut down of internet connectivity or phone networks was rarely deployed before the rise of mobile media. With the mobilisation of computing the interaction with and through digital technology increasingly abandons the separation between the physical and the virtual – for instance when technology becomes smart and location aware (such as GPS, NFS, Bluetooth or wireless LAN). But how are locative technologies able to have a political impact?

Geo-referencing media technically works everywhere, but the content it produces is location-bound and dependent on a specific place as Thielmann and Döring have shown.[4] Think for example of tracking and tracing systems such the street-toll system in Germany or remember that you increasingly see location specific status updates generated by geo-referencing tools in your Facebook timelines. Those location specific variations imply that digital and physical space are no longer separately organised but relate to each other. Digital codes and physical traces increasingly create a hybrid form of spatial representation, one that connects data and places and includes the location specific action of their users. In other words, territoriality becomes constitutive for our forms of social interaction and the configuration of political participation.

Take Sukey as an example beside many others: Sukey is a platform designed during the 2010 UK student protests to keep people safe, mobile and informed during demonstrations. It crowdsources information from online and offline sources such as Twitter or SMS to provide protesters with a real time overview of what is happening around them. Users can anonymously upload photos and text reports or tag tweets which are then structured and fed back to the platform. It seems as if this type of location-based data mining does not just apply to our digital footprint like communication profiles, travel logs, access control systems or payment methods but that online protest engages just as well with technology in ways that sets up new and hybrid forms of agency.[5] Not only do mobile phones know where we are,

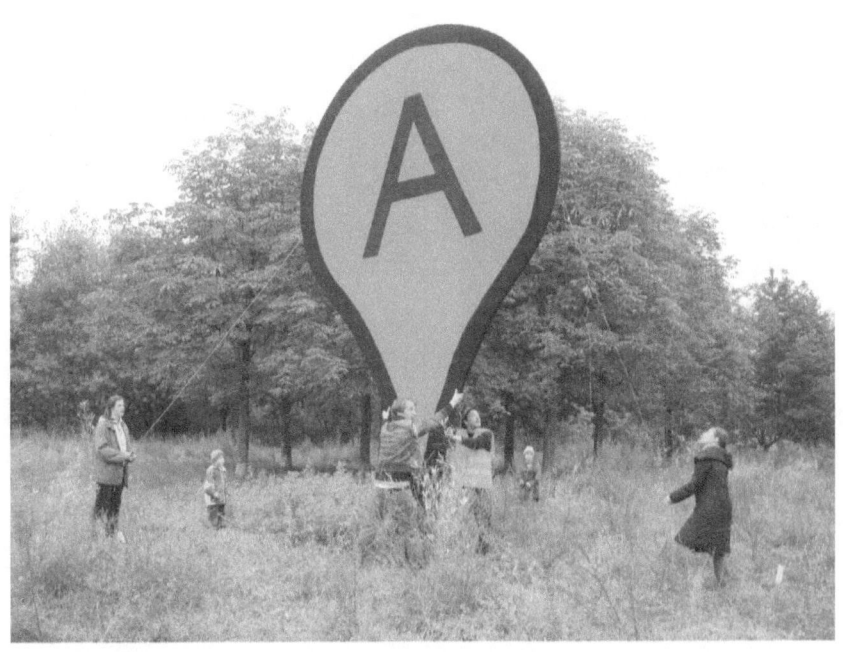

Aram Bartholl, *Map*, 2007

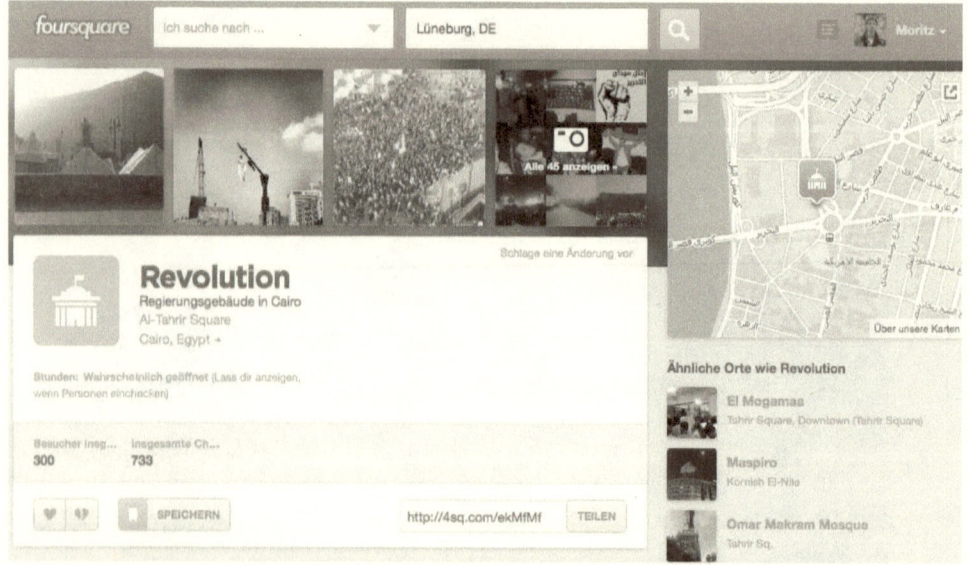

Screenshot of Foursquare check-in on Tahrir Square, https://foursquare.com, 2013

where we have been and even where we are most probably about to go next, riot navigation systems also guide us safely through demonstrations, just as hashtags are filtered according to their location, GPS chips add geolocations to our visual status updates or location based surveillance technologies (such as most smartphone apps) recognise us according to our use of technical devices. It seems like we might check-in a revolution on foursquare just as we lifeblog workout runs.

Obviously, the political actors of a digital society no longer separate 'the internet' from 'the streets'. Instead the development from the isolated mass media spectator to the post-media networker of tactical technology integrates virtual and real forms of political participation. While the forms of political protest dissociate from the concept of the virtual, our interaction with and through digital technology becomes increasingly socially integrated and spatially contingent. Territoriality has finally become a kind of authorship and our movements themselves are turning into a political practice. The social graph that we so desperately try to resist might indeed be increasingly correlated with a place graph. But the loss of individual autonomy that we experience when using services like Google or Facebook might be accompanied with new forms of crowdsourced and collective agency that create new places and disclose a new kind of spatial experience.

Footnotes

1   fffffat 2011
2   See respectively, Richard Smith, 'The End of Geography and *Radical Politics in Baudrillard's Philosophy*', *Environment and Planning – D: Society and Space*, 15(3), pp.305–320 and Vilém Flusser, 'Das Verschwinden der Ferne', *Archplus*, Jg. 24, Nr. 111, 1992, pp.31–32, Paul Virilio, *Speed and Politics: An Essay on Dromology*, New York, 1977.
3   Respectively, Sherry Turkle, *Alone Together: Why We Expect More from Technology and Less from Each Other*, New York, 2011 and Evgeny Morozov, *The Net Delusion: How not to liberate the world*, London, 2011.
4   Jörg Döring, & Tristan Thielmann (Eds.), *Mediengeographie*, Bielefeld, 2009 and fffffat, 'Occupy the Internet!', 2011, http://fffff.at/occupy-the-internet/
5   Editors' note: for criticisms of Sukey in the UK context see the Libcom forum thread, 'Sukey Sucks', http://libcom.org/forums/general/sukey-sucks-09022011 and Random Blowe, 'The Curious Case Of Sukey And The Bizarre Press Release', http://www.blowe.org.uk/2011/02/curious-case-of-sukey-and-bizarre-press.html

LIFE VS. OBJECT, COMRADE THINGS AND ALIEN LIFE

The flattening out of ontological hierarchies between humans, animals, machines and objects is a characteristic turn of postmodern philosophy, science and arts. This flattening challenges the enlightenment subject as the fulcrum of cognition and action in order to admit alien ontologies into formal understandings of the world and its production. Object-oriented ontologies, from Actor Network Theory to Speculative Realism, are shaping research methodologies, computer science, network cultures and government. Aesthetics, which finds its origins in the relationship between human sense-perception and the experience of beauty, is likewise shaken by the intensifying proliferation of non-human ontologies and/or extension of non-human perception and production, its distributed systems and scales.

How might radical social perspectives interpret these convolutions of thought and action which reconceive human and object relations? How do current models of politics contend with the question 'do artefacts have politics?' How do we relate digital aesthetics – in which abstract computational actors like algorithms give rise to new forms and morphologies – to the social and sensuous conditions in which they arise and take effect? What happens to our understanding of politics and culture when the satisfaction of 'human needs', however problematic these are to define, ceases to be a key aim of knowledge systems? What, indeed, is 'thought' when the notion of the human, let alone the cogito, is recursively destabilised by the same man-made tools developed to defend our ontological centrality and certainty? What can we make of 'cognition in the wild', when 'the wild' is seen not as threatening or dystopian, but as a social utopia?

MAPPING THE CONJECTURE

FABIEN GIRAUD

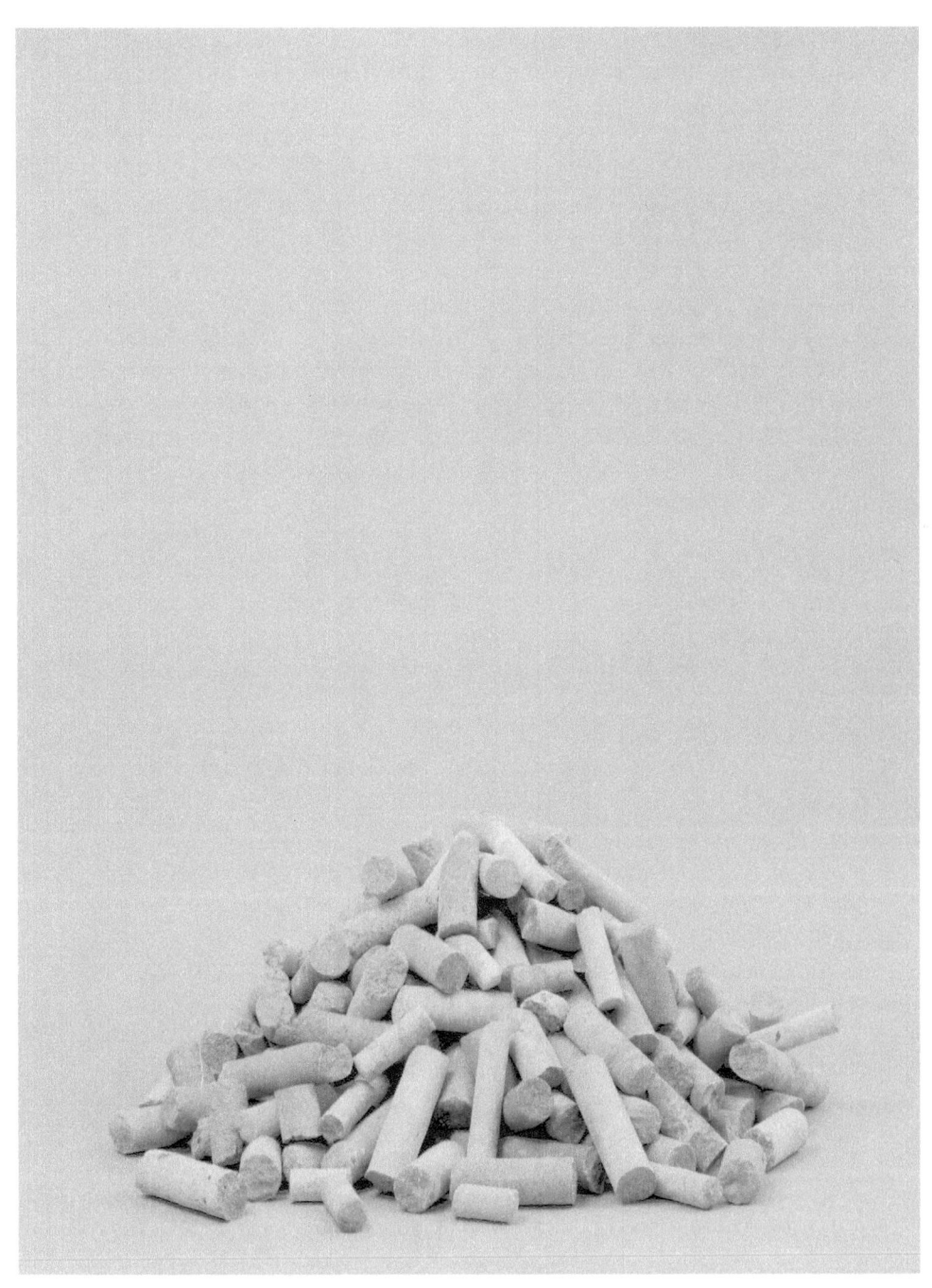

Fabien Giraud, *The Marfa Stratum*, 2013

It has become quite evident for many of us today that the geological concept of the anthropocene represents one of the most useful contemporary notions to depart from the scepticism of postmodernity. The Matter of Contradiction work group which I co-founded in 2011 attempted to address this notion in its most acute definition and wide ranging consequences.[1]

Departing from its strictly geological definition, the anthropocene has become for us a possible way to rename modernity itself and thus come to terms with the infinite and desperate adjunctions one could add to the era (post-, trans-, alter- modern, etc.). To put it very simply, the anthropocene is a geological concept which takes into account man's recent influence on the planet's formation and integrates it as an era proper to the general timescale of terrestrial history. The argument put forward here is that since the beginning of the industrial revolution in the late 18th century men cannot be considered as simple inhabitants of the earth any longer but as full actors in its material becoming.

As a result, it can be argued that the strength of the anthropocene concept lies in its paradoxical value. On one hand it puts the human at the centre of a world in which fate becomes irrevocably bound to our thoughts and actions, on the other hand it collapses the human onto an equivalent plane with geological entities and movements, where our gestures become no different in kind to the tectonic activities in the earth or the sedimentary processes in rock formation.

This movement of collapse and the subsequent disintegration of the ontological boundaries upon which our knowledge of the world had been based creates a kind of epochal panic. One where the sealed epistemological realms come to vacillate under the pressure of this newly ungrounded ground. In response to such a panic, one can schematically identify two main tendencies – two different definitions of the theoretical conduct to undertake in the midst of the panic and the blurring of all categories: *relationism* and *eliminativism*.

These two positions create a clear bifurcation which seems to resonate in most of contemporary discourses and practices. Relationism, which is best represented by flat ontologies and actor network theory, can be roughly defined as an attempt to use this situation as a way to overcome or simply reconcile the foundational cut at the beginning of the modern era. If indeed, we have never been modern, it is, from the view point of relationists, because any separation between man and nature, concepts and objects, stones and thoughts, are nothing more than woven fictions we have invented for the purification of an ever more mixed and transient world.

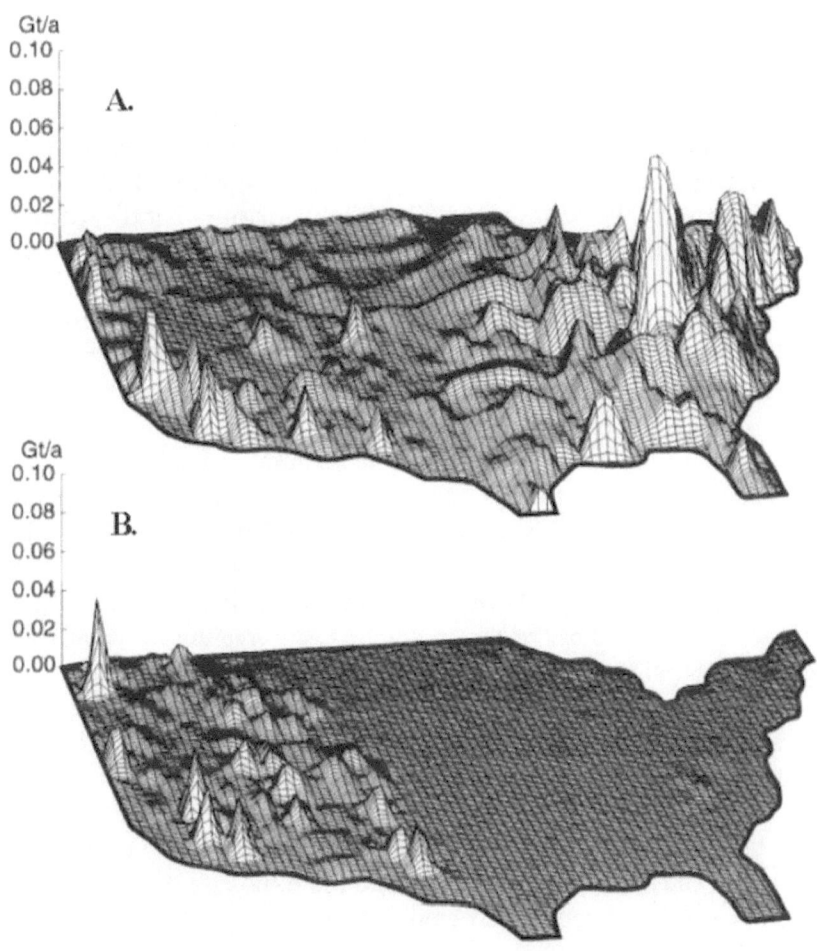

Earth movement by humans and rivers. Maps of the United States showing, by variations in peak height, the rates at which earth is moved in gigatonnes per annum in a grid cell measuring 1° (latitude and longitude) on a side, by (A) humans and (B) rivers. Hooke (1999).

Eliminativism, on the other hand, is based on the pursuit of radical naturalism – an agenda which prolongs the modern gesture of the cut by an ever increasing objectification of thoughts and processes. If, to paraphrase Patricia Churchland, we are nothing more than thinking meat, our aim should not be to safeguard the priority of meaning over sheer indifferent matter but rather to deepen and strengthen the decentering consequences of its investigation.

What is common to both approaches is an attempt to renegotiate the way we inherit the foundational dialectical gestures of the modern era. However, by placing us in an alternative between the 'vivification of stones' (relationism) or the 'stonification of life' (eliminativism) what they actually do is to prolong further the very foundations they mean to overcome. This alternative between a concept infused object (relationism) or an objectified concept (eliminativism) belongs indeed to the exact same logic – they are actually two sides of the same coin – one which takes for granted a certain conception of the separation between the concept and the object as a disjunction in the real. An ontological rupture folding back any approach to anthropocenic panic to a preconceived philosophical decision.

The synchronous though conflicting emergence in contemporary aesthetic and political discourses of neo-primitivist and accelerationist positions seem to prolong yet again the same philosophical determination. The accelerationist escape plan from the future dead lithosphere and the neo-primitivist safeguard of the benevolent Gaia converge in the symmetrical and reversible affects of global desolation and local sustainability.

Far from living up to their promise of overcoming the panic of our times, their dialectics between an ultramodern leap into the void and the reclaiming of a premodern fabric serve nothing else than to reinforce the sense of a lost epistemic ground which has long disappeared from under our feet.

The question at the basis of my research is to find a way to overcome such dead ends: it is an attempt to find a route through the panic which would be true to the opportunity brought about by the anthropocene.

Formation / Formalisation

What is required for such a task is, I believe, a shift from the standard concept/object dialectics to the dynamical weaving of *formations* and *formalisations*. Under this standard conception, an object is already a cut made by the concept: it is always pre- and over- determined by its act of decision

Plants, Androids and Operators

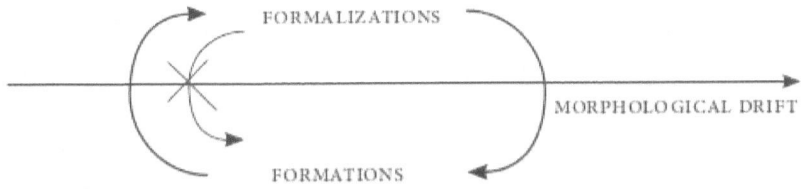

Fabien Giraud, *Formalisation/formation model*

on the real. What we propose instead is a distinction between formations – as all formal processes independent of the meaning we attribute to them – and formalisations – as all formal productions attempting to make sense of formations.

By formation, we should understand any kind of processes which lay outside the realms of significance – a voluntarily vague notion encompassing the full spectrum of material movements radically indifferent to 'Being' as such.

By formalisation, we understand the wide range of actions within and through formations made by certain beings in order to construct and unfold the minimal condition of a world. These gestures are not the irreducible property of man but cover a wide gradient of possible worlds – a scope which comprises just as much animal strategies of predation as abstract movements of intuition in human mathematics.

However, this shift must be made carefully so as not to fall back into the reversible dialectics it tries to depart from. That is, even though all formalisations are constituted of formations, all formations cannot necessarily be formalised in return.

In other words if all formalisations can be naturalised (i.e. considered as formations) the inverse movement is not necessarily true as it would imply to force meaning through the indifference of formations (such a forcing which is recurrent in certain 'relationist' philosophies).

A formalisation is never retroactive upon formations, it cannot reverse the current flow of formations without taking the risk of essentialising indifferent processes, attributing intentions or principles to the muteness of inorganic and organic processes.

The anthropocene opens this model to its fully non-linear, non-deterministic nature: instead of a reversible movement between stones and thoughts, processes and meanings, it unfolds as a constant positive feedback

Mapping the Conjecture

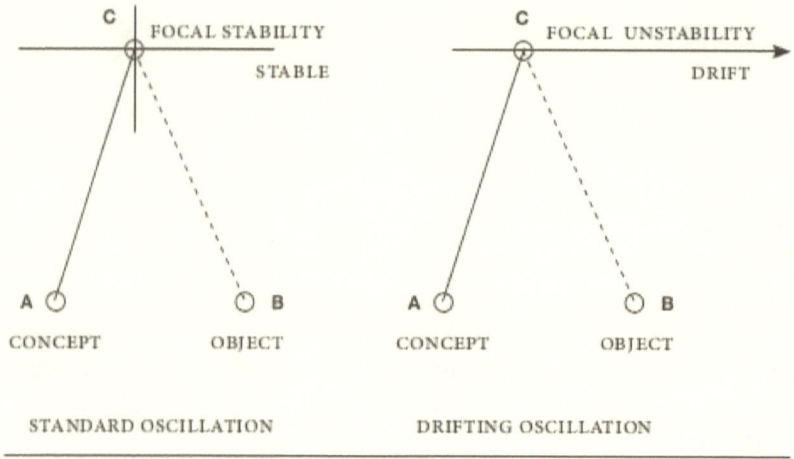

Fabien Giraud, *From standard 'stable' oscillation to 'drifting' oscillation*

loop between formations and formalisations – triggering non-reversible drifts of the entire system (as entropic transfers from formalisations come to alter radically the grounds of formations). This morphological runaway is what triggers the true panic of the anthropocene: cognition can no longer claim the safe place of the concept in opposition to the object but must confront itself to its full embeddedness in the drifting contingency of formation and formalisation movements.

Mapping the Panic

The precise mapping of such a panic is the current focus of my work. Instead of the incessant reversibility of its divided terms, the formation/formalisation couple unfolds as a continuum of constant morphisms between constitutive polarities. As such it cannot be thought of with the common tools of 'flat ontologies' as such theories already posit the planarity of a standard surface on which to unfold their model. What we need instead is the schematisation of our contemporary landscape as a non-orientable surface: a plane where the act of decision between sides is rendered impossible by the structural continuity of its faces (the Moebius strip is obviously the most famous example of such a non orientable surface – but many others are conceivable). The constitution of such a space is not a new theoretical ornament to add

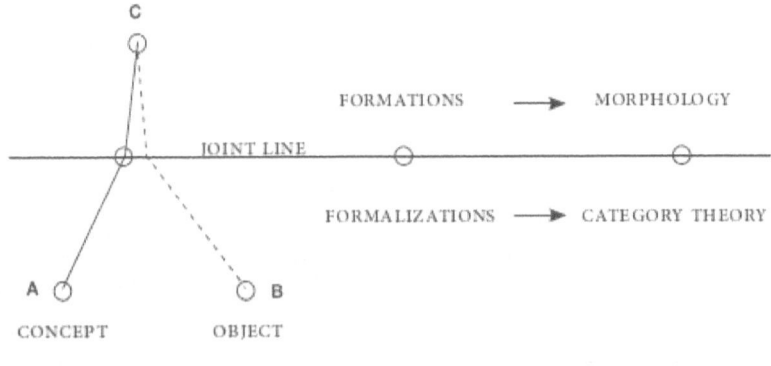

Fabien Giraud, *Double pendulum model between formations/formalisations*

to the chains of concepts in the midst of a panic but the proper terrain of our contemporary landscape. A terrain which has to be carefully analysed and described in order to act within it. I conceive this approach as a kind of articulation of two models coming from contemporary mathematics one is the morphology of René Thom and the wide ranging semiophysics which emerged out of it, the other is category theory and the Grothendieckian geometrisation of epistemology.

This being the heart of my present research, I will only sketch out here the overall dynamics at the basis of this ongoing enquiry. For that I will call to an experimental diagram which hopefully will give a clear idea of this ground of investigation.

If the concept/object dialectics is conceived as a pendular motion between two poles, the formation/formalisation couple stands for the oscillation itself. The 'phase-space' which maps its intricate movements constitute the terrain of our contemporary landscape. How the pendulum came to be constituted is a 'morphological' problem – the kind of epistemic space which unfolds through its oscillation is a 'categorial' one. In other words, if morphology is the logic of formations, category theory is the logic of formalisations. The following diagrams and examples try to approach the way they might be articulated.

The pendulum model is made of three elements: the position of the Concept (A), the position of the Object (B) the attachment point for the pendulum itself (C). If we consider a fixed attachment point (c) its Focal Stability in dynamical system terminology then the movement of oscillation between the Concept (A) and the Object (B) is constant. It can easily be transferred (through a series of plottings of positions and momentums of the pendulum through time) on a two-dimensional phase-space mapping the entirety of its possible behaviours: a deterministic phase diagram where any points in the system can always be deduced from the others.

However, if the attachment point of the overall pendulum is no longer fixed but 'slides' along an invisible axis, the behaviour of the overall system is entirely affected – it triggers a series of unpredictable movements which reconfigure entirely the phase-space landscape. This 'sliding focal instability' at the origin of the oscillation is precisely the kind of contingent morphological drift revealed by the anthropocene.

Such a sliding of the attachment point being difficult to picture, we can schematise it as some kind of double pendulum where the transition between logics of forms and epistemic categories are jointed together in a doubled oscillation movement (keeping in mind that this simplified model is necessarily incomplete as it implies a kind of infinite regression: a loose attachment point is always preceded by another fixed and stable one, etc.)

If the constant articulation from formations to formalisations and the subsequent transfer of movements from the morphological to the categorial had to be plotted on a diagram representing the global behaviour of the system, the resulting phase-space would unfold as a seemingly chaotic system.

The approach of such a complex epistemic landscape resulting from this double oscillation and the possibility to act upon its formations is the focus of my work. I consider this work not solely as a standard mapping or diagnostic analysis of our present but as the unfolding of a practice of art as 'embedded navigation'. Such an approach requires a renewed conception of navigation itself, one which would not only be a means for circulating through the map, but the properly immanent practice of reshaping the very terrain on which it relies: a practice of art as a continuous invention of tools and vehicles for the 'terraformation' of our epistemic landscape.

Navigating the Panic – Glass Bead

If The Matter of Contradiction work group and its three events (Art Without Esthetics / Ungrounding the Object / War Against The Sun) was conceived as the diagnosis of our anthropocenic condition and the mapping of its conjecture, the Glass Bead project is a laboratory for the invention of new ways of navigating through its landscape.[2]

Co-founded in 2013 and planned to be operational in the spring of 2014, Glass Bead is an international research laboratory, a journal of art theory and an online survey of new ways of instituting in the anthropocene.

Loosely inspired from the eponymous book by Herman Hesse (*Das Glasperlenspiel*, 1943), where an order of intellectuals at the start of the 25th century play an abstract game of synthesis of all types of knowledge, The Glass Bead project proposes to transfer and take on the experiment in our contemporary world.

Just as category theory in contemporary mathematics is a rigorous investigation of abstract spaces through an immanentisation of its own logic, the 'game' as we understand it is above all a constant invention of its very rules for experimentation. The only common ground for the game to start is the shared will among 'players' to start the game.

The origin of glass beads might be traced back to the middle of the desert, millions of years ago, where columns of hot air rising from the ground forces moisture to ascend through the atmospheric layers. The accumulated pressure in resulting convection currents find a sudden relief through the electrostatic discharge of a thunderbolt. When lightning hits the sand, the immediate temperature rise breaks the bonds in its material structure. Chunks of quartz melt, and petrified by instantaneous vitrification, leave a lightning glass imprint into the sand.

Maybe it is by imitation of this fulguration process, maybe by accident, that someone took out molten silica from the heat of a kiln and poured it into a stone mould, and while cooling it and rolling it in between his fingers, made of the resulting sphere the unit of reason which launched the game.

Glass beads are built through a synergy of practices and forces, they are as much the product of weather conditions, technological actions and geological movements. They are entities of human and non-human constitution. When they started rolling from the Mesopotamian desert to the Scandinavian plains, through processes of pairing, ordering, comparing and trading as ways of measuring and reasoning with the world, they merged the materiality of their constitution with the abstraction of their movement. As such, a glass bead is precisely one of these joint balls between formations and formalisations. They stand on the articulation line of transfer between morphologies and epistemologies. They are both the unit of the game and the plateau for the unfolding of its actions.

The aim of the Glass Bead International Research Laboratory is to find new ways of navigating through the heterogeneity of epistemic landscapes. In order to do so, it is conceived as a collective confrontation with the concept of locality. A locality can be anything from a geographically grounded situation, a specific conceptual construction or a tonal inflection in contemporary harmonics. Each one of these localities is a particular Glass Bead which connectivity with the others is never pre-determined but has to be carefully assembled through collective inventions of modes of navigation. A Glass Bead is never a discrete point in and of itself. It is always the product of a local/global relation - the unfolding of a thread between the 'here' and the 'there'. The invention of navigational routes between Beads implies the careful weaving of these threads in order to constitute the singular fabric of these epistemological grounds.

The laboratory itself is organised on an annual cycle of investigations of such localities. Research groups are formed by inviting a wide variety of people from different fields of knowledge to work on site. Each Glass Bead constituted by the group during the session is then 'poured' on the connectivity field to interact with other Beads. Beads on the connectivity field are then worked and morphed to constitute larger Beads thus launching an avalanche process of successive formal inventions at all levels of the experiment.

The annual journal operates as a cut in the process of connectivity between Beads - presenting a phase in the continuous morphing and ever growing experiment. For the year of its launch the laboratory has planned to work in Laboratoires d'Aubervilliers, France and at PS1, New York, USA.

Morphing Vehicles - The Marfa Stratum

The Marfa Stratum is an ongoing project made of two distinct elements - a series of sculptures in the region of Marfa, Texas, in the form of synthetically aggregated core samples speculating on the geological becoming of human formations, and a book (in collaboration with Ida Soulard) unfolding the complex dynamics which have come to constitute this particular human event stratum.

The town of Marfa is located in the middle of the American Chihuahuan desert of West Texas. Since 1974 when the minimalist artist Donald Judd came to settle in and install his permanent collection, the ghostly town swept

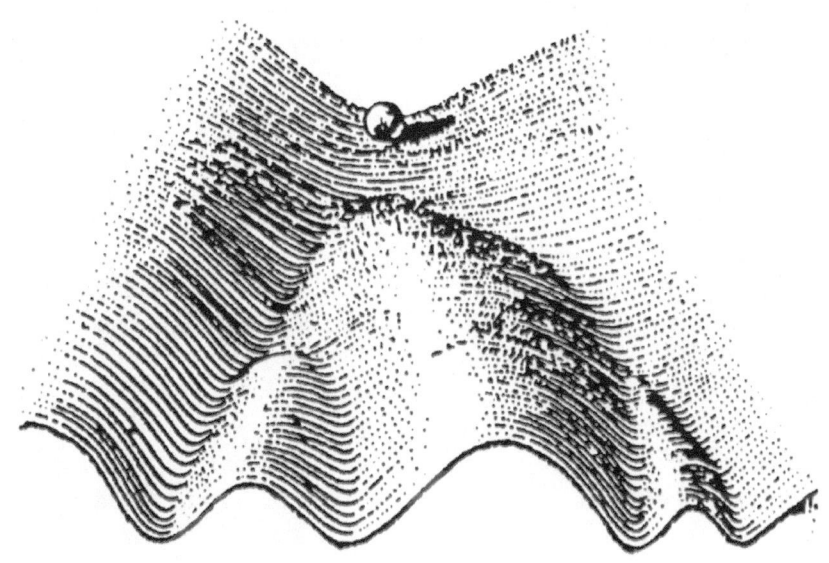

Conrad Hal Waddington, *Epigenetic Landscape*, c.1946

by arid winds has progressively become one of the most visited locations on the international art map. Forty years later, the proliferation of galleries, art residencies, restaurants and the subsequent real estate inflation have 'permanently' launched the gentrification process.

If Donald Judd is renowned as the symptomatic promotional figure of site specificity and context related art, our work was initiated as a question concerning the status and validity of such a concept under the contemporary condition of the anthropocene. Marfa as an urban island surrounded by desertified eroded plains has come to incarnate the localisation of such an idea on the epistemic landscape. This overlapping of geography and epistemology reveals the site specificity of Judd, not so much as an inscription of works of art in relation to a natural environment, but as a confirmation of a predetermined locality of the concept.

Such determination and strict localisation has been rendered impossible by the anthropocenic conjecture – a conjecture where art can no longer be defined as an exceptional territory in the pre-mapped lands of epistemology, but as a venture exploration into the unknown of drifting knowledge grounds.

Entrada was the term coined by Spanish conquistadors of the 16th century and described by Charles Nicholl as a journey where 'you left the margins, the settled, the known and made your *entrance* into that unmapped interior where just about anything was possible'.[3]

In Marfa, the axiomatic monsters of the cartographies of conquistadors are here replaced by neoliberal chimeras wandering in the immaculate oil innervated white cubes of art institutions. From the deflagration of cocaine infused dopamine in the brain of international curators to the cognitive erosion of the anthropocene, this book is both a grotesquely realist epic of neoliberal art and a practical manual about how to build escape vessels out of its stasis.

If site specificity can no longer be reduced to the locality of a concept (the specificity of one philosophical decision) and our discontinuous epistemic landscapes are made of heterogeneous and often incompatible terrains, then, the vessels we have to build to navigate through them should be of a morphic nature. Their construction has to take into account the impossibility to rely on an equivalence of the locality to the globality and must integrate in their structure the potential morphisms they will have to undergo.

It is our claim in The Marfa Stratum that the only true 'specific site' of today is located on the deck of such a vessel.

Engines of Connectivity

The contemporary call to the figure of the mesh, the web of relations, the rhizomatic landscape have come to structure the underlying foundations of most of our contemporary political visions. The network is the generic horizon shared by both neoliberal economism and leftist sustainability. It might even be that these precise political positions have become irrelevant precisely because they share this same epistemic ground.

A network is always already a decision on a type of relations, it is a decision on a specific universe, the anchoring of a distribution between localities and globalities. The contemporary alternative between a thriving global economy and the alternate safeguard of local markets seem to be nothing more than a reassuring fiction in order to avoid a true confrontation with the epistemic deadlock of the network.

How can we conceive of modes of connectivity which do not pre- or over- determine the relations between the multiplicity of its constitutive localities? How can we conceive of connectivities as heterogeneous 'trail lines' between an infinite modulation of local/global relations?

Here again the articulation between 'morphology' as ways of thinking through a radical naturalisation of epistemology and the Grothendieckian architecturing of topoi through the epistemic landscape should be the main theoretical framework for this investigation. Once again, it should unfold as an articulation - a constant movement of transfer between logics of formations ('morphologies') and logics of formalisations ('categories').

Politics of the Network

The 'network' is a type of formalisation which has come to dominate all others thus blocking the political potential of imagining the possibility of other worlds.

On one hand, Grothendieckian topoi theory (literally: a theory of the possible) will help us to reposition networks among the plurality of all possible epistemic universes. On the other hand, morphological conceptions of cognition as understood by René Thom, Jean Petitot or Giuseppe Longo will help us unravel the ways in which such a form of cognition has emerged out of natural processes and series of evolutive bifurcations.

It is self-evident that our understanding of the concept of a 'network' and the political gestures it triggers are largely based on the contemporary

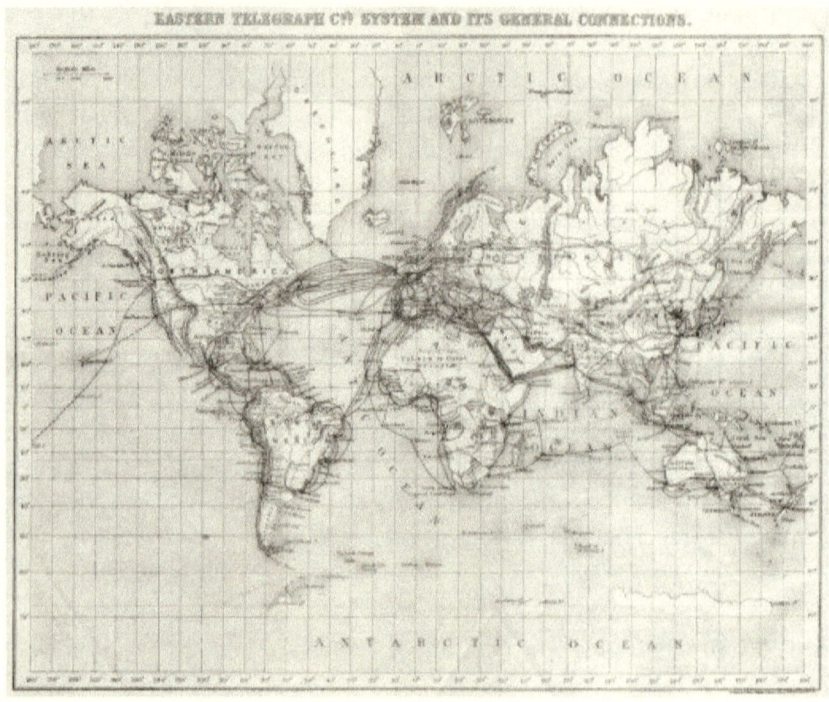
World map of submarine telegraphic cables, Eastern Telegraph Company, 1901

apprehension of discrete state machines (as Alan Turing initially named the modern computer).

An investigation of the network as the dominant political epistemology should therefore concentrate on the proper fabric of this constraining landscape and from there envision ways to reshape its terrain.

Following our axiomatic doubled pendular motion, it should:

1. Try to see how discretisation has been cognitively inferred from the continuum of morphological processes.
2. Try to understand to what extent this categorical determination can be put in relation with other possible categories and thus transformed through a series of homotopies and continuous morphisms.

Finally, if the discrete engine is the political reason of our times, it should speculate on a new kind of engine capable of altering its proper model of functioning – a modal engine for cognition, equipped with a hybrid motor fuelled by the constant transfer from formations to formalisations, categories and morphologies, and thus capable of launching the new modes of navigations required by the anthropocene.

Footnotes

1   *The Matter of Contradiction* was co-founded in 2011 by Fabien Giraud, Sam Basu, Ida Soulard and Tom Trevatt. Inigo Wilkins joined in 2013. All material related to *The Matter of Contradiction* can be found here, http://lamatiere.tumblr.com/
2   *Glass Bead* is a project initiated by Fabien Giraud and Ida Soulard. The directors and curatorial board are Fabien Giraud, Jeremy James Leconte, Vincent Normand, Ida Soulard and Inigo Wilkins.
3   Charles Nicholl, *The Creature in the Map (A Journey to El Dorado)*, Chicago: The University of Chicago Press, 1997.

STACK, HEAP, FRAME

MARTIN HOWSE & JONATHAN KEMP

Inactive Frame N-7

Stack is nature. To heap is human. The frame is brilliant, paranoiac cosmology.

The Cretaceous follows the Jurassic as an eye-eroded bit pushed onto a shift register.

Where man is not, nature is barren.

We know with the frivolity and shallowness attained only by the playing card depth of any tawdry scenery.

We inhabit a land of stacks and heaps and frames and pitfalls and dire mills.

This certainty, of reason, has never been made evident in nature as some kind of message graven in stones or in the earth itself.

Engineering is only the fulfilment of a logical operation on the landscape; a making of a monument to reason, a walled garden.

No environment, only an unvironment.

How it comes to pass that there can be the idea of something hidden in the world?

Nature as a stag(for)-loop for a bachelor (party) machine.

There is never a 'we' which creates, regards or has anything to do with any world, solely a bare existent which is handed down, a scraping child storage and investment. This is culture. To make the world always the same again and again.

A mockery of layerings and geology. The rocks are never to be left alone, never to be washed or wind swept; the world could at least be drowned.

The world is an island existing only to utter endlessly the absolute clarity of the fact that there is no exterior; that all physics is endophysics.

Stack, Heap, Frame

This is the death of earth.

Hydrating the dead with their fluid logics.

Inactive Frame N-6

Bootstrapping a mud mind based only on the sheer flatness of stack and heap diagrams, and other falsified hierarchies.

There is nothing encrypted that will not be decrypted, nothing hidden that will not be made known.

The universe is like a vast frame whose innermost dungeon is the earth, the scene of man's life. Within it the cosmic spheres are ranged as in a nested call-return stack, growing downwards. Belief in any science implies a belief in contained reason and thus sheer religion.

The bounded is loathed by its possessor. The same dull round, even of a universe, would soon become a Turing tar pit of ever more complicated instruction sets.

Stack of manias, heap of shit, frame of blood.

A question of how a reality as experienced by this species is held as the individuation of a set of possibilities in the context of a mountain slope of increasing entropy, with no potential appeal to any enclosing daemon.

Shift the fog-bound or waxy instruction pointer completely into the outside.

Logic attempts the domestication of the material in that it normalises elementary particles: matter is broken up into universal elements according to the double bind of the contemporary frame: position and motion.

Life and death are passive, distinguishable only when pulling at the frame.

To give direction to death, it is all the logic of the sacrifice, of the execution ritual.

At all times the planet dies and is reborn, one moment to the next in a blind blizzard of mini-deaths.

Inactive Frame N-5

Ontology is a container question, best left for those in any containing world.

Cruelty is the mirror of philosophical determinism.

Code is a play between an ontology of hiding and a functionality of revealing which is in one sense the world (given in that decision making) as a military/philosophical project of a holding of the day and of the world as (un-)certain.

There really is more of everything.

Every thing in this world is more sluggish than its neighbour; easily condensed and more ready to fall prostrate in the face of your earth.

The world is packed with mutant certainties, thrusting to become and remain temporarily as they are. 'Anything does not go' – some aggregates and associations are forced to the front, and others ultimately fail; so nothing here for the piss prophets to read.

You are nothing but a heap of earth. The problem is not that the learning curve is so flat; the problem is that your slope is so negative.

The revelations of hidden strata, attuning rocks to humans; these are the carry outs fashioned from the cuts made into the Universe by its vertiginous schizophrenic subjects.

Obsessed with how words relate to things or how the mind represents the world, working back and forth between crumpled thought experiments and the smooth space of text, you systematically translate and distort yourself and the earth.

Terrestrial thought depends on the memory of the sun, buried thought depends on the memory of the cosmos.

Stack, Heap, Frame

Abbreviated mammoths, flickering switches, ablated minds.

There are always two forces which serve to hold everything together in its own proper connection and proper form, as the strata and the limit of the literary palaeontologist's regard.

Inactive Frame N-4

I demand an auto-poetic conspiracy, with neither theory nor grounding, a two-dimensional demarcation of paranoia which forms an absolute boundary; everything is connected *only* within these bounds.

The Time Traveller arrives in an empty landscape, littered with monuments, decoded and open to any meaning. He experiences a false and shoddy sunset as in a story but with the self-awareness on his part of that total crudeness. The Time Traveller reveals the truth.

There is little choice as to whether to live within a contained world.

Any enclosure is defined by the clear exposure of a constructed boundary condition; for example, the camera keeps on rolling, affording a view of the reality behind the scenes of that particular 'construction'.

The fact of this enclosure renders all humanity absurd.

Certainty is completely barriered against demonic entropy, tracing a harsh world-line.

That which simply cannot be executed, which refuses to be executed in the world as it is.

Enclosure is the foundation of abstraction and language; a theatre of cruelty and of leakage.

All is hidden. All will be revealed (by accident).

Geology implies a false beginning which cannot be thought as it implies a boundary.

Instead of always a pornographic image, 'they' make it on the surface itself. Instead of always a screen, a stage for icons and faked openings, there is a piercing of the flat surface.

There exists the lack of any definition but sheer certainty.

Psychozooism is modern anti-romanticism.

Every action supposes contained symptoms: footprints, fingerprints, text, chromosomes, o's and 1's. So no layer of soot from worldwide conflagration, no layer of salty, bubble-free ice from a giant wave; nothing so cruelly irreducible.

Inactive Frame N-3

If fundamental technology is like the plague, this is not (only) because it is contagious, but because it is a revelation, urging forward the exteriorisation of a latent undercurrent of cruelty.

When you will have made of itself a technology without components, then you will have delivered it from all its automatic reactions and restored it to its true freedom.

Like the plague, technology is a crisis resolved either by death or cure.
Sexual desire is never anything but the possibility computers have of combining and exchanging their signs.

You see me completely naked.

Pornography is the pure foundation of computation and execution.

Abandon stratification; computation has absolutely nothing to do with geology.

How can it be that any crash is always tearfully faked and falsified?

With every (computer) crash, the programmer should be forced to drag her fingers through the earth endlessly.

Stack, Heap, Frame

Technology buries humans alive in order to re-place the site of execution under the earth. This is the sole 'reason' for technology. There is no other. This conspiracy is revealed by software operating under the codename 'Poe' and further obfuscated by softwares reciting the name of any 'philosopher'.

To conceive this life sacrificed in the mort/court-circuit, the machine logic of sacrifice.

All these dendritic exchanges, stacked, stored, all combined in the same operation of artificial insemination and premature ejaculation.

It's not just that the question of calculating; in this *mise en scène*, the distance between the dead writing and the living reader. More, it's a question of highlighting the irreducibility of the play within the electronic system, to exceed its movement, accelerate its cycles until saturated, constrained in an urgent tautology (the assertion of the assertion).

The electronic circuit = electric circuit + Input/Output. The double bind of death and life, a rhythmic interval in its real.time I/O, excluding the not yet births and already done (to) deaths.

Computation compels us to search for signs, not of some more vital reality, the ruse of the earth, but of the absence of its own ceaseless revolution (the ironic trajectory of its particles and the chaotic turbulence in its material systems).

To assume a reality that is polygonal because a model is elegant or intelligible is plainly absurd, to assume a reality that is polygonal because a model is elegant or intelligible is plainly absurd.

Inactive Frame N-2

Computation stands barely against an impinging animism or entropy gradient which knows of no enclosure, of no cell walls, of no disciplines which might name this or that process as electronic, as physical, as biological, as belonging to this or that domain; a promiscuous stupidity, waving its less-than-located-neural-branches.

The blind or feint of the operating system is to define itself 'as an interface between hardware and user', and thus between users, when all its work and energy (from the world) is spent on a functional set of abstractions (all code), of enclosures and on the separation of effects, of love.

Infect. (Copy). Execute.

How to transfer execution across materials and against containment?

That there can be a hiding for which execution can be a revelation.

The most terrible crash is the one that does not reveal its symptoms.

Software exposes the world in the way it holds itself as certain.

There is no software, only vampiric execution on some kind of earth substrate.

Engineered code is a simultaneous hiding and revealing in a failed attempt to contain against contamination and infection.

How can a quine become manifest in geology or in flora?

The gate, in the asymmetry which it poses (a closed gate opens onto nothing), activated by the 'fairy electric', incarnates symbols to be locked up in the rhythms of ritual exchanges (violence, murder, intrigue).

The vulgarising of the earth in the binary of the logic gate by supposing the transfer of charges in a system of material energy carried in and out from zero value. Zero is wedged into hardware to exist in its literal read/write, an effect of the flat *trompe l'œil* of language, locked up in a circuit where the promised play of neutralising the earth as superfluous is contained.

The false logic of where the instruction wants that which is given, is never returned.

The computer says: 'I will automate your logic' and the logic says 'I will tell you what your programs mean'.

Stack, Heap, Frame

Inactive Frame N-1

The mystery is precisely how quotation is embodied in hardware, how a statement which can talk of other statements can become part of the unreadable earth.

The historic, plague ridden for all times, story of the long wait for the rendering executable outside the magical, for the modern Enigma, ends now with a blank refusal of the execution of all things, of the word made promiscuous flesh.

Crash *is* the site of execution of language.

Faust specifies that the 'characters of signs' force the spirits, just as for Turing it was the teleprinter.

Forever conjoining with the play of symbols; limed in this dead reality, they never left the place where they were made to be.

The confinement of the spirit of this logic inside what is a nicked mineral stack can be brought closer to the ritual conspiracies of demons, or pacts with the devil.

When you construct something like a computer, it's thanks to an idealism contained in desultory turns: computers are made of circuits, and circuits render symbols, and symbols bear meaning.

The read/write head gives life to the dead symbol, at the price of the excluded human middle. Quotation is nothing but fantasy.

Inactive Frame N

Thinking is always falsely stratified and arranged. Words croak with a mantled crust.

Thinking is to be dragged in reverse from absolute animism all the way back to the Cretaceous. Unburying or violently expulsing a stack overflow or extinction event.

Thought can give only after it has received, by itself it is nothing but an empty heap.

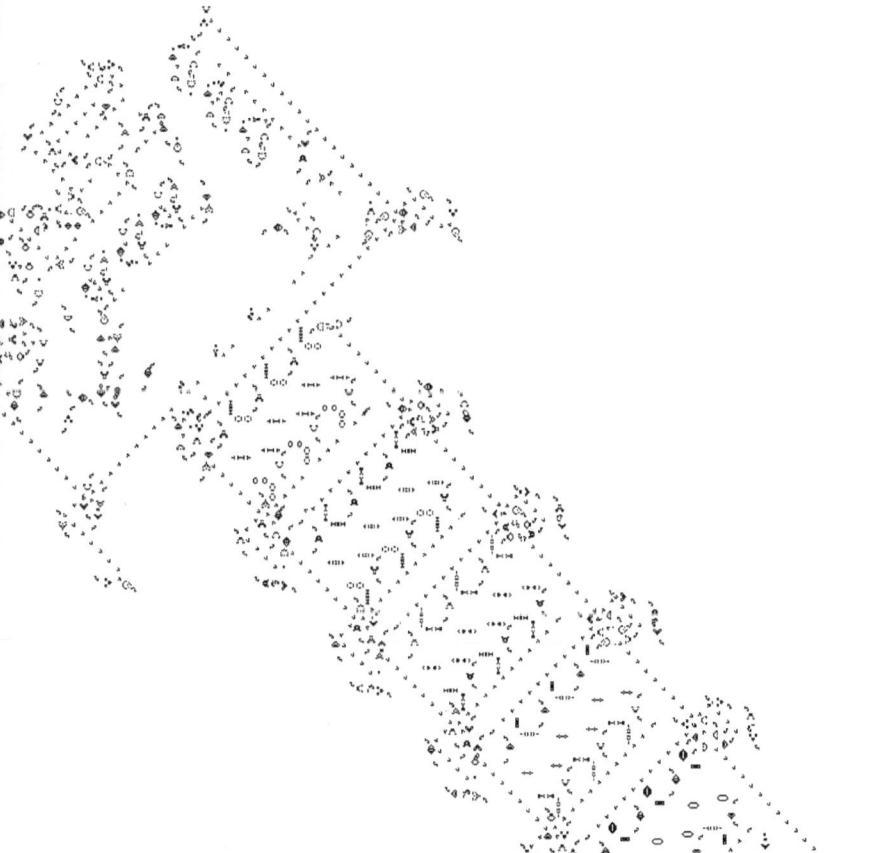

DECKSPACE.TV RESYNCED DIARIES

ADNAN HADZI & JAMES STEVENS

Deckspace.TV is a SPC collaboration with Post Media Lab and presents an audiovisual management and publishing system representing collective processes and media production of SPC subscribers in Deckspace media lab from the last decade.[1] It functions as an open, collaborative system that facilitates artists, film-makers, researchers and participants of its workshops to store, share, edit and redistribute media.

The open and collaborative nature of the Deckspace.TV project demonstrates a form of shared media practice in two ways: audiences become producers by managing their material, and contributors are able to organise their productions and interact with each other. This research operates in the context of a European political discourse concerning countercultural approaches to non-mandatory collaboration and contractual agreements.

Deckspace.TV productions are made available with an open content license such as the Free Art License, the Creative Commons SA-BY License, and the GNU General Public License.

Wilderness

On Friday, 11 October 2013 we held the first of a series of reSync workshops in Deckspace, 'Wilderness', where we reviewed tools for collaborative video production, considered how best to construct reports, and investigated the mechanics of Bit Torrent Sync (BTSync) in preparation for inclusion at future workshops. We began at noon with a run through the objectives for the workshops and how we might sequence explanation, interaction and expression of the key activities successfully. This included developing an archaeology of SPC resources, review discoveries and published reports along the lines of the heap, frame, stack motif proposed by Jonathan Kemp and Martin Howse.[2]

Since then some preparation has been made to pull together disparate media files from the many Deckspace workstations and external hard disks, and from the webservers that host a mass of video, image and audio data. Adnan Hadzi has already engineered a collaborative process for film-makers at Deptford.TV, which we have utilised to annotate, store files and author fresh compositions.[3]

We authored our own BTSync install recipes for Linux, Windows and Mac OS users as we felt the available guides fell short in some respects. After installing the available BTSync software onto desktop, laptop and portable devices, we experimented to discover how best to operate the various options, improve communication of the P2P sharing concepts and implement BTSync. We used print media to carry the NFC and QR code that links to the report and associated media resources.

We identified the following case uses:

Scenario #1: Mobile user wishing to sync files.
Scenario #2: Laptop user offers sync to local files.
Scenario #3: We offered a read-only sync folder on our server and synchronised between laptops on our LAN and mobile phones via 3G operators.

Transmissions

During a reSync workshop held on 18 October 2013 we studied the mechanisms for broadcast we have made use of over the years. We welcomed Anthony Davies from MayDay Rooms and missed out on talking to Bruno Sanhueza, DJ TechNoMore contributor to the WirelessFM we host at our stream server.[4] When we first opened Deckspace in 2001 several of our longer term collaborators from Backspace were keen to continue with their live audio and streaming projects.

PirateTV presented live streaming video and audio from their original home at Coldcut studio in Clink Street, where they were based until 1999, and from their later location Outerbongolia in Herne Hill, South London. <Blink> was featured in a touring Arts for Networks exhibition and utilised the pioneering Frequency Clock engine designed and built by Adam Hyde.[5] He installed a Frequency Clock for <Blink>, which we used at Deckspace for many years. Jem Finer authored Longplayer, a thousand year musical composition driven by SuperCollider scripts to celebrate the millennium. SPC has hosted the listening station since 2002 and we have worked with Longplayer Trust to keep the composition publicly available.[6]

A Pirate Radio Listening Station was designed and built by Heath Bunting and moved to Deckspace from the ICA in 2008.[7] It lists pirate radio FM broadcasts receivable in the SE London area and allows remote control of the tuner, which in turn re-streams the selected station. In 2010 Rob Canning installed Sourcefabric's Airtime server, but so far we haven't turned to it as a tool. It remains available at our airtime server.

We have been discussing which of the newer solutions could be of use to us as we review the SPC repository we are building at Deckspace.TV. We

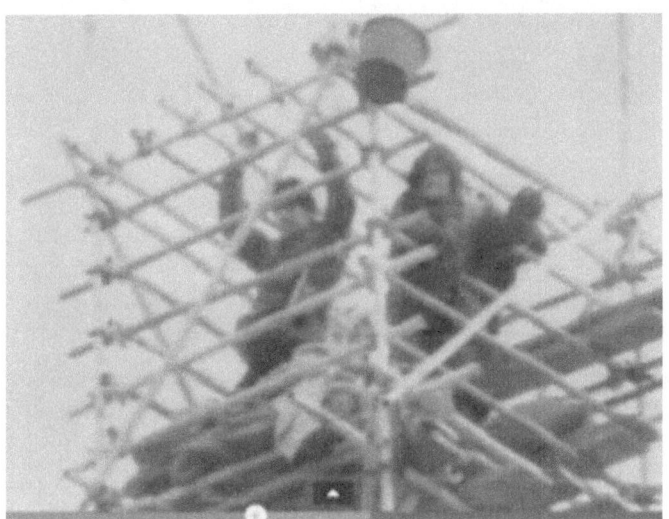
Pirate TV still image of the M11 protest, 1997

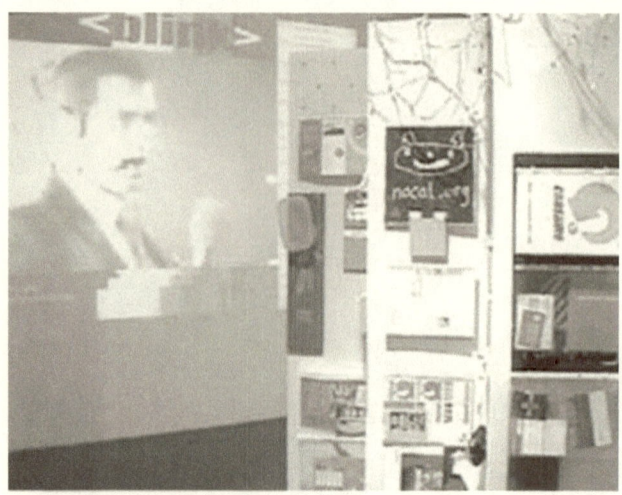

OWN installation, DMZ conference, Limehouse, 2003

like Pad.ma for its ability to manipulate metadata and accommodate 'deep links' into the timeline.[8] InterLace by Robert M. Ochshorn takes these ideas further, incorporating slit-screen views of film strips and contextual interlinking in its web-based player.[9]

During the session it became clear that our enthusiasm for BTSync would present issues for our project as it is not open source so we looked at alternative methods of P2P transport for our report publishing. Giovanni d'Angelo turned up as we began this discussion and suggested we look at Retroshare. Adnan already had an install of Owncloud operational so he issued us accounts to test out.

Rights

This year's Mozfest, 29 October 2013, was again held at Ravensbourne College of Art adjacent to the O2 Dome in North Greenwich. Every view from the portholes inside was a reminder of the spectacular transformation of the area since the start of the new millennium.

One of the attractions for us this year was the formal unveiling of the Firefox phone but after the opening night it was in little evidence. Instead the focal point was maker badges and the mushrooming interest and utility of Webmaker products. One of these initiatives set out to prepare specifications for a Webmaker teaching kit with kids and beginners in mind.

Security and safety on the web was of course a theme on everyone's mind this year. The series of crypto workshops were well attended and explored how to use PGP for email, public key encryption tools for messaging, and Tor for web browsers. Those of us with smartphones installed and configured 'ChatSecure' for Android.[10]

Objectives

Due to circumstances quickly changing, the week's workshop turned into a radical real-time performance. The object facilitating this was a parcel sent by Julian Assange to Nabeel Rajab.[11] This performance nicely fitted the theme of the fellowship – Life vs. Object – with the fourth research cycle 'Life versus Object. Comrade Things and Alien Life' focusing on the flattening out of ontological hierarchies between humans, animals, machines and objects, and the new parametric realities brought about by networked media environments.[12]

Origins

We set out to explore the material archive we have at Deckspace for the print, image and online records relating to SPC's origins. Backspace was open and operational throughout 1996-2000, a period which primed us for so much we have experienced in the years that followed. Independent media production and political action gained new strengths from internet based communication and we all experienced the dynamism of the rush of attention towards some of the work we produced as well as the realities of regeneration in the inner cities that eventually closed the space. Before that moment passed so much flowed through, around and over us on its way towards the future it was hard to capture and take it in at the time.

Javier arrived bang on time for the start of a session at 11am, 9 November 2013, so we had plenty of opportunity to discuss current work and indulge in a little nostalgia for 1999-2003 during the early days of Indymedia London and our adoption of Linux.[13] He is currently a campaigner at the Open Rights Group as well as helping establish a bilingual free school in Brighton demonstrating an enduring enthusiasm and commitment to a wide scope of civic and political action.[14] The following data dump of what's new, related and essential in the field of archivism, rights and digital activism took place in a stream of consciousness hard to account for now. We certainly talked a while about DIY book and newsprint scanners and the Free Births, Deaths and Marriage register projects.[15]

One activity in the workshops was digging through the accumulated archive boxes containing, posters, flyers and stickers for the J18 Carnival Against Capitalism. This crowned a golden period in Backspace when it was used as the first ever Indymedia Centre, from where a coordination of videos arriving by cycle courier from the City of London actions were streamed to the world's public via SPC servers.

Giovanni d'Angelo was one of the key Backspacers back in the day and also joined us again for further excavations as we distilled the stored materials into specially cleared shelves in preparation for closer examination and processing. Before long, tables already loaded with lunch debris are joined by contents of the CD racks and VHS silos. The Art for Networks boxes brought up from bitspace featured OWN (in it's earlier form as POD toolbox), <Blink>, our iteration of Frequency Clock and Consume the Net. All of these were all featured alongside many other contributions in an exhibition curated by Simon Pope in 2002.[16]

Adnan brought along a newly acquired NFC/RFID tag writer for miscellaneous cards and stickers we have yet to activate but which form the publication and promotion component of our research program. Alexei Blinov, a long term collaborator at SPC and instrumental to so much technical practice and support to so many, arrived to remind us of his Broom project which utilised similar RFID readers and to help us round off the day's work with beer before joining us at an Exploding Cinema show in Brixton.

We discussed the GCHQ/NSA big data gathering concerning the change within legislation. The Criminal Justice Act, which was introduced 10 years ago by the British government in order to prevent free parties and festivals and which initiated a mass movement of resistance culminating in J18. Mark Harrison stated in an interview with Neil Transpontine, that 'the Criminal Justice Bill was rushed in – and this drove much of the dance music scene back into the hand of The Industry'.[17] Might Eben Moglen's Freedom Box be a way out?[18]

Screens

16 November 2013. Our efforts to date have allowed us plenty of opportunity to re-familiarise ourselves with events and productions at Deckspace

and we continued digging out materials. James Braddell joined us for the start of this session on his way out to Rome. It was a great opportunity to discuss some assumptions about the value of archives and practical issues of identifying, processing and representing moving image work. Much of his work expresses a wry sense of humour and explores the structures of music with texture and imagination. His latest video work *City* concentrates dense HD into immersive environmental compositions.[19]

For more than two decades Exploding Cinema have held open access screenings where thousands of producers make their films public for the love of it. Their zine-style show booklets and posters pepper the whole archive. In 2005 the world began to turn in their home movies, cat fetishes and music videos to YouTube and since then billions pour their daily lives into the stew of social media silos. In the end we have all been compromised by universal self and state surveillance.

By this point there had been some breakthrough progress on our efforts to install InterLace as Robert Ochshorn had a bit of time to refine his codebase and get a version working for us. There is a growing range of similar web browser based playback systems available which we will continue to make use of and explore.[20] You can now review some of those SPC DV archives we already spent so many hours digitising but never edited. Inter:ace opens in a web browser and lays out the film strips end to end down the page. To activate the viewer click any clip and presto, like dropping the needle on a record. Each clip is then accessible for metadata tagging, interlinking and dynamic reordering by category and context.

Rachel Baker arrived at one session in time to find us winding up the day's work and reflecting on these screens, origins and objectives and had a lot to offer from her own experiences as member of Irational.org but also as early contributor at Backspace. She is currently working with Booksprint and urges us to produce a printable set of these notes as part of our workshops![21] This 'Screens' workshop session also marked the 10th anniversary of the 'DMZ' festival organised by Armin Medosch in 2003.[22]

Futures

23 November 2013. In the final reSync session in the UK we focused on 'futures'. It was a very cold day with the wind blowing around the roof which perhaps put some people off. However it was great to welcome Paolo Cardullo and Atau Tanaka. Paulo is a photographer and cultural

studies tutor currently working on proposals for a Deptford walking/map project with the British Library Archives fund, so we were able to confer techniques for street signage with QR codes and NFC to promote linking and syncing of pictures and maps available. Atau Tanaka is currently Professor of Media Computing at Goldsmiths leading a five year research project at the Embodied Audiovisual Interaction group.[23] There are some great opportunities for the use of NFC and QR codes in music yet to be explored as well as a wealth of new media systems now available to aid experimentation such as eMotive.[24] In 2008 Cardiacs frontman and creative powerhouse Tim Smith suffered a catastrophic stroke, which left him with impaired voice and motor function.[25] Atau confirmed his department had research and practice commitments for just this sort of disabled support in terms of music making which may lead to some well needed support in 2014 for Tim. Gargi Sen from magic lantern movies arrived later in the afternoon to discuss new approaches to the distribution and presentation of documentary film archives, which deserve greater development and reward.[26] They are in the process of applying for the NESTA R&D fund for the Arts to develop a documentary film distribution platform for cinema audiences.

Freifunk

13 December 2013. A workshop in Lüneburg featured a great Freifunk presentation by Hauke who lives locally and hosts an access point at his home in the centre of the city.[27] We discussed the many aspects of free network infrastructure and how the local group collaborates to present open access. They run a flavour of Freifunk software that tunnels all the IP traffic crossing the network to a Swedish internet gateway thus navigating the Störerhaftung or 'Secondary Liability' laws otherwise limiting open hearted Germans at home.

Under each Freifunk sticker is now a RFID tag you can scan with your NFC capable smartphone to open the BTSync point, which holds the workshop documentation. You will need BTSync installed and internet connection to activate this link.[28]

We all considered prospects for future collaborations and infrastructure building with Freifunk, interlinking Post Media Lab, Freiraum and Stadtarchiv which would be attempted in time to coincide with the Taking care of Things conference in January 2014. The workshop concluded by warwalking about the city on the hunt for Freifunk wireless networks,

Freifunk Bittorrent Sync Sticker, Lüneburg 2014

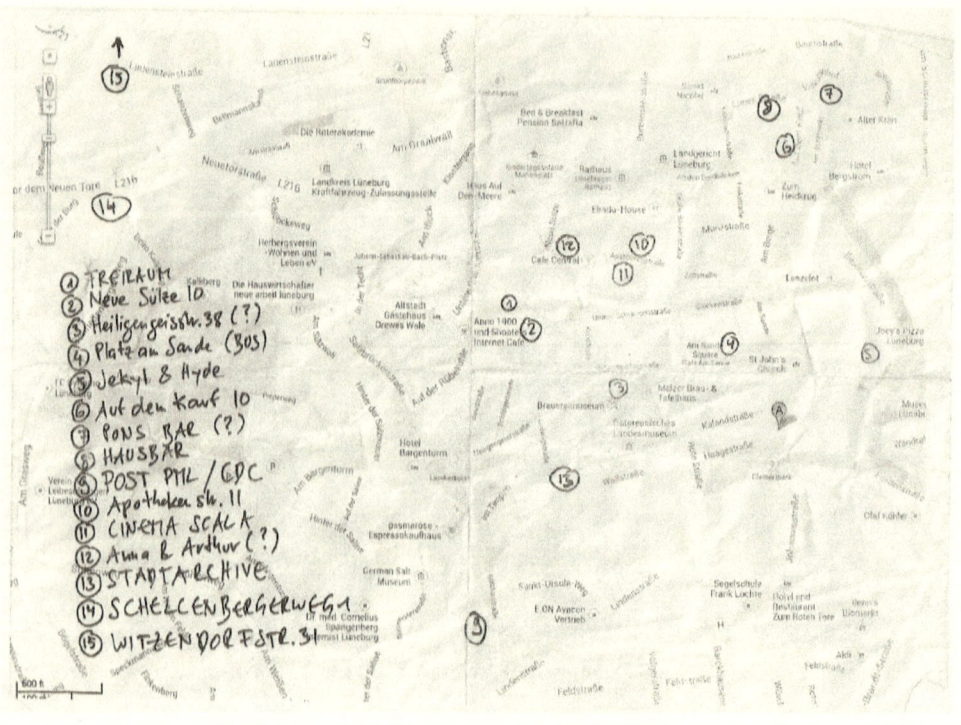

Map of ReSync operations, Lüneburg, 2014

which we celebrated with the QR codes, stickers and NFC tags as described above.

Graswurzel

14 December 2013. Graswurzel.tv has been active since 2006 when they first got involved in filming political actions and publishing their documentaries. Founders Suze and Marco attended the Saturday workshop at Freiraum Lüneburg to present a potted history of their group activities. They showed us some of the many accounts of actions during a very busy five years.

More recently they have been mapping the resistance to open cast mining of lignite in the far East of Germany at the border with Poland where devastating environmental damage across a vast area is ongoing in the quest for cheap energy.[29] Thousands of residents have already been decanted to other areas and mining has lead to the disappearance of entire villages.

We discussed how the evidence of these and other campaigns is often buried in the weight of information accumulating from often lengthy campaigns. Later in the afternoon we turned to the second task of the day to prepare a live Linux 4 gigabyte USB key for video editing uses and re-purposing a small NAS unit to serve as a reSync host for data there at Frieraum once we left.[30]

Freiraum

15 December 2013. During the final workshop day we met again with Alexander, the CEO of Freiraum, who has been our primary contact and host the three days. He presented an account of establishment and development of Parklokal foundation and illustrated the many areas of activity and ongoing engagement with business and community that have developed since. We heard (Wall 2013) about their beginnings at Hausbar and progression to music venue Salon Hansen leading to addition of Freiraum itself and introduction to Lunatic Festival.[31] Max is a student at Leuphana University and the outgoing chair of Lunatic. He talked in animated terms about his experiences working for the festival, detailing the educational aims and commitment of the university to maintain support of this very successful student run event. The recent addition of arts exhibits at the festival has opened up new opportunities for engagement and involvement of the local

community of Lüneburg. We collated this workshop report and produced a fresh set of QR codes and NFC stickers set to link back to an online page hosting this support. These linkable stickers were fixed to windows and walls in the district.[32]

Footnotes

1   For more about Deckspace, SPC.ORG, http://dek.spc.org/
2   See 156-165. in this volume.
3   http://deptford.tv/
4   http://airtime.kiben.net/login
5   BLINK - Direct Access Media Channel, http://dek.spc.org/blink/ Frequency Clock, http://radioqualia.va.com.au/freqclock/
6   http://longplayer.org/
7   http://scanner.irational.org/
8   http://camputer.org/event.php?id=7
9   http://opensourceecology.org/wiki/InterLace
10 See https://guardianproject.info/apps/chatsecure/
11 See http://wikileaks.org/rajab
12 The parcel left the Ecuadorian Embassy on Monday the 28 October with the Twitter status: 'Sending Nabeel Rajab a parcel containing a camera. Camera documents its journey through postal system in realtime' We only received a few decipherable images, then the camera went blank and only black images were transmitted (we speculated that the camera might have been put into a bag). Furthermore we seemed not to move at all, and were stuck in the Parcelforce depot for over a day.
    On Tuesday things moved, and the parcel was transported to Stansted Airport but not with the hoped outcome of being transported out of the country; on the contrary, after another day of waiting, the parcel was brought back to the Parcelforce distribution centre in Camden.
    After not moving for another day !Mediengruppe Bitnik started to enquire into the whereabouts of the parcel and received conflicting status messages from Parcelforce and FedEx. Bitnik tweeted: 'FedEx says parcel it's at Parcelforce – they say it's at FedEx. Our GPS says: http://goo.gl/maps/jbvPK'. After this tweet, things suddenly seemed to be moving (if it was because of this tweet we shall never know). WikiLeaks' response to this was:

> One can imagine the politics as the political hot-potato parcel is thrown between Royal Mail, Parcel Force, FedEx and UK Customs. No one wants to be left holding the parcel if a story breaks about refusing to let it through to Bahrain's top political prisoner.

The Parcel left the country on a flight to Paris on Thursday night, the 31 October, 2013. It only stayed at the Paris airport for a few hours before being loaded onto a flight to Dubai, where it arrived Friday morning.

Plants, Androids and Operators

Another day passed.
Unfortunately we permanently lost the connection with the parcel on the 2nd of November at around 9AM (GMT). FedEx changed the tracking status of the parcel to N/A, and !Mediengruppe Bitnik tweeted:

24'010 live images | 23'626 black images | 5594 km | 6 days | 6573 GPS readings | 3 countries | 3 airports | #postdrone

#Postdrone from Assange to Nabeel Rajab was stopped at Dubai Airport. But our journey to Bahrain is not over yet. Stay tuned for updates.

13 For more about the Independent Media Centre Indymedia, see http://docs.indymedia.org/
14 Peter Bradwell, 'Rights holders' proposed voluntary website blocking scheme', 2011, http://www.openrightsgroup.org/blog/2011/rights-holders-propose-voluntary-website-blocking-scheme
15 http://www.freebmd.org.uk/
16 The Art For Networks exhibition was held at Chapter in Cardiff, Wales, http://www.chapter.org/art-networks
17 Neil Transpontine, 'Spiral Tribe Interview with Mark Harrison', *Datacide*, no.13, October 2013.
18 Eben Moglen, FreedomBox Foundation, see https://www.freedomboxfoundation.org/
19 A preview of *City* can be viewed online, http://www.youtube.com/watch?v=paUoUFQ_QwY&feature=share&list=UU2PG3kgbPh7C7Q1XsFvrKFQ&index=3
20 For example *Montage Interdit* by Eyal Sivan, http://montageinterdit.net/
21 Booksprints, http://www.booksprints.net/
22 http://dmz.spc.org/londonzip.html
23 Embodied AudioVisual Interaction Group, http://eavi.goldsmithsdigital.com/
24 http://www.emotiv.com/
25 http://www.cardiacs.net/
26 Gargi Sen and Magic Lantern Movies, http://magiclanternmovies.in/director/37
27 Hauke Winkler's presentation is available, http://filmcode.org/deckspacetv/wp-content/uploads/2013/12/reSync-Pr%C3%A4sentation.pdf
28 BTSync://BGDWMQW7IJMWRBZYEBGSZ2CU3CQKC6LMH
29 Graswurzel.TV, http://www.braunkohle-tagebau.de/
30 BTSync://AMXG3ZTOOSBO6CXCJYPFSRDQCQ4FEKQ2N
31 nformation on these projects can be found, http://www.salonhansen.org/, http://www.hausbar-lueneburg.de/ and http://lunatic-festival.de/
32 Here is the BTSync secret AX65KPZECNZC3U37KNEVEHVPSNWVGSWXJ please use it to synchronise your device.

CONTRIBUTORS' BIOGRAPHIES

CLEMENS APPRICH studied Philosophy, Political Science and History in Vienna and Bordeaux. Since 2008 he has been a PhD-student in Cultural History and Theory at *Humboldt University of Berlin*. He was a Junior Research Fellow at the *Ludwig Boltzmann Institute for Media.Art.Research* in Linz as well as at the *Institute for Human Sciences* in Vienna. He was actively engaged in the media art initiative, Public Netbase, and is still affiliated with the World-Information Institute.

From 2009 to 2013 he was on the editorial board of the Austrian journal for radical democratic cultural politics, Kulturrisse, and is a co-founder and editor of Kamion, a transnational journal for political theory, artistic practices and critical thinking. He has been a guest lecturer at Goldsmiths College in London, and is teaching at the *Institute of Culture and Aesthetics of Digital Media (ICAM) at Leuphana University in Lüneburg*.

In 2011 he co-founded the Post-Media Lab at the Centre for Digital Cultures (CDC) at Leuphana University in Lüneburg, which he has been coordinating since then. He is also a member of CDC's *Steering Committee* and coordinating editor of the web-journal, spheres. Affiliated with the *Digital Cultures Research Lab* (DCRL) he is currently working as one of the Principal Investigators of "Making Change", a joint research project between the *Centre for Digital Cultures* and the *Hivos Knowledge Programme*.

JOSEPHINE BERRY SLATER is Editor of *Mute* magazine, and a co-ordinator of the Post-Media Lab, Leuphana University. She teaches part-time at Goldsmiths on the Culture Industry MA and an option course in Biopolitics and Aesthetics. She is also co-author, together with Anthony Iles, of No Room to Move: Radical Art and the Regenerate City.

MICHA CÁRDENAS is an artivist, hacktivist, poet, student, educator, mixed-race trans femme latina who works at the intersection of movement, technology and politics. Micha is a Provost Fellow and PhD student in Media Arts + Practice (iMAP) at University of Southern California and a member of the art collective Electronic Disturbance Theater 2.0. Her co-authored book *The Transreal: Political Aesthetics of Crossing Realities* was published by Atropos Press in 2012. She has presented individual and collective work at museums, galleries and biennials around the world. She holds an MFA from University of California, San Diego, an MA in Communication from the European Graduate School and a BS in Computer Science from Florida International University. She blogs at michacardenas.org and tweets at @michacardenas <http://twitter.com/michacardenas>

SEAN DOCKRAY is an artist living in Melbourne, Australia. He is a founding director of the Los Angeles non-profit organisation, Telic Arts Exchange and initiator of global platforms The Public School and aaaarg.org.

RÓZSA FARKAS is founding director and co-curator/editor of Arcadia Missa Gallery and Publishers in London. Her research fellowship at Leuphana University's Post Media Lab explored affect after the internet. Farkas' curation and writing spans across Arcadia Missa's projects, as well as external projects such as a curatorial residency for tank.tv, and texts for organisations including .dpi Feminist Journal of Art and Digital Culture, Mute magazine, and Nottingham Contemporary. Farkas is guest lecturer at University of the Arts London. http://arcadiamissa.com/.

ADNAN HADZI undertook his practice-based PhD in 'FLOSSTV - Free, Libre, Open Source Software (FLOSS) within participatory 'TV hacking' Media and Arts Practices' at Goldsmiths, University of London. Adnan's research focuses on the influence of digitalisation and new forms of (documentary-) film production, as well as the author's rights in relation to collective authorship.

MARTIN HOWSE is a programmer, writer, performer and explorer occupied with the question of where exactly software or code executes. For the last ten years he has collaborated on numerous open-laboratory style projects and performed, published, lectured and exhibited worldwide. Recent projects and performances by Howse and Jonathan Kemp have been informed by an interest in code-brut reconfigurations of computation's material substrates (eg. The Crystal World, Psychogeophysics).

ANTHONY ILES is a writer of criticism, fiction and theory. He is Deputy Editor of Mute magazine http://metamute.org and a co-ordinator of the Post-Media Lab.

JONATHAN KEMP has a long history of elaborating situational events as active makings-in-the-world. Project collaborations (including ap and xxxxx) involve material processing performances, environmental installations, experimental communicative systems, and social software events, executed throughout Europe, Brazil, and the US. Current projects and performances are informed by an interest in aleatory and code-brut reconfigurations of computation's material substrates. In 2013, he was awarded a PhD in Experimental Media Arts by the University of Westminster, London. http://xxn.org.uk http://crystalworld.org.uk

OLIVER LERONE SCHULTZ is one of the initiators of the Post-Media Lab. Before his work at the Center for Digital Cultures in Lüneburg, he spent several years of engagement in media- and video-activism, as well as in graphics, media conception, documentary and curtatorial work. During this time he also conducted academic research on media theory, embodiment, cognition and recently on intervisuality. He is also engaged in the conception of trans-academic events, like Video Vortex #9 in 2013. Currently he is one of the Principal Investigators of 'Making Change', a project of the Common Media Lab engaged in building a 'knowledge-commons' methodology and scrutinising intersections of mediatised culture and conceptions of social change. http://lerone.net

MORITZ QUEISNER is a media studies scholar who investigates the relation between digital media and the transformation of social interaction. He works as a research associate at the Cluster of Excellence Image Knowledge Gestaltung of Humboldt University Berlin. Queisner is a member of the Collegium for the Advanced Study of Pictureact and Embodiment and has been a fellow at Post Media Lab at the Center for Digital Cultures, Leuphana University Lüneburg. His PhD project 'Augmented Vision' is associated to the research training group Visibility and Visual Production: Hybrid Forms of Iconic Knowledge at the Institute for Arts and Media of the University of Potsdam.

GORDAN SAVIČIĆ is a researcher and Critical Engineer. The main research areas explored through his projects include game cultures, digital and urban interventions, architecture, pervasive computing as well as open source technologies. As a practising media artist he has exhibited projects and performances throughout Europe, Asia and South-America and received various awards. His fellowship at the Post-Media Lab revolved around the question of where Reasonableness and Seamlessness meet?

JAMES STEVENS is the founder member of SPC and lives with his family in Deptford SE London. Whilst directing operations at web boutique Obsolete in 1996 he launched Backspace, the proto cybercafe on Clink Street, London Bridge; a response to conversations with artist Heath Bunting on the needs for an accessible place to explore creative networking and critical media in public. It became a touchstone for a thousand web coders and inventors, and inspiration for the technology spaces and businesses that boomed in the years that followed. James teamed up with Julian Priest in 2000 to present wireless network primer Consume which advocated the open wireless networking that today thrives at OWN based in Deptford SE8. SPC moved up to Deckspace in 2001 and retains the rooftop studio spaces for use by its subscribers and continues to offer DIY web, mail and media hosting alongside a bramble of experiment and collaboration in progress.

INIGO WILKINS is in the process of completing his doctoral thesis on the topic of 'Irreversible Noise' at Goldsmiths' Centre for Cultural Studies, where he explores the philosophical implications of the concept of noise as it has been developed in the sciences. He is co-director of the arts journal *Glass Bead*, has published articles in *Mute* magazine, and has given numerous talks relating his research to a wide range of subjects, including aesthetics, politics and economics. His research fellowship at Leuphana University's Post Media Lab focused on the subsumption of sociality.

www.ingramcontent.com/pod-product-compliance
Lightning Source LLC
Chambersburg PA
CBHW020655220526
45464CB00001B/440